Winging it!

'WHAT'S DONE IN LOVE
IS DONE WELL'

VAN GOGH

Published by Lagom,
An Imprint of Bonnier Publishing
The Plaza,
535 Kings Road,
Chelsea Harbour,
London, SW10 0SZ

www.bonnierpublishing.com

Hardback – 978-1-911600-01-5
Ebook – 978-1-911600-02-2

Designed by Sophie Yamamoto / Maru Studio
Printed and bound by UAB Balto Print

1 3 5 7 9 10 8 6 4 2

ALEX JONES

winging it!!

PARENTING IN THE MIDDLE OF LIFE!

LAGOM
BOOKS FOR A BETTER BALANCED LIFE

This will probably be my first and last book so...
to my boys, Charlie and little Ted. My parents, Alun
and Mary and my sister, Jennie.

CONTENTS

INTRODUCTION

The tweet went out. Alex Jones is releasing a book about motherhood.

Cue the furious tapping on keyboards:

'Not another one sharing her so-called baby tips?'

'What does SHE know about bringing up a baby?'

OK... hands up... I admit it... Nothing! Not a clue. My sister and my best friend both bought me the sweatshirt you see me wear on the cover last Christmas, which pretty much summed up how they thought it was going to pan out – and they were spot on. Hence the title. Truth be told, I'd never even changed a nappy until I had Teddy last year at 39. Before then, I thought that swaddling was something they did to baby Jesus back in the day, but wasn't 'a thing' any more. Now that I've spent 12 months being responsible for a small human there are a few tips that I could share with brand-new parents – nothing ground-breaking or life-changing, just some handy suggestions, parent-to-parent. This book is not a guide or a parenting manual, because, let's face it, that ground has been well and truly covered. I see this book as more of a conversation starter or a support group, if you like. A place for parents who have had their first child in their thirties and forties to get together and celebrate that we are procreating later in life, while working out, with the help of some proper experts, the best ways of integrating a new addition into a life that is already nearly at capacity. I searched for this sort of book when I was pregnant. A book that I could connect with, that spoke to me as a working mother in her late thirties; and I didn't find anything that quite hit the mark, so I've had a go at writing one.

THE QUESTION

Let me share a bit of my back story. Charlie, my husband and I got married on 31 December 2015 and four minutes after the ceremony, Auntie Marian led the charge with: 'So are you going to start trying straight away?'

It was challenging at times

Bless Auntie Marian, but I'm sure most of you, having been there yourselves, will share my irritation, to put it mildly. In the weeks that followed, the same question was fired at me at least once daily, mainly by journalists, who usually followed up with 'Are you worried you've left it too late?' I always gave a breezy answer, but in reality I was going through life in a state of low-level irritation, which was mostly fuelled by unhelpful headlines in the papers like these:

FEMALE FERTILTY CLOCK STARTS TICKING AT 27!
FERTILITY WOES OVER 30!
FERTILITY RATE FALLS OFF CLIFF AT 35!

I wasn't paranoid, but I had become increasingly curious about the impact of age on our fertility. I trawled the internet but comprehensive information on the subject was hard to find. I wanted to challenge these ageist headlines, see for myself how closely related age and fertility are, and I wanted to meet others who were about to embark on parenthood a bit later in life so that we could compare notes.

> 'There's definitely a generation gap with being an older mum – my mum was in her early twenties when she had me, and our experiences are totally different because of that, from how our bodies are to our jobs; I don't feel like I have a touchstone – we really are winging it!' Jenny

Television is flooded with documentaries on various health topics such as how much we drink, how much red meat we eat, insomnia, dementia and how to stay young, but there is little airtime given to arguably the most important of all: fertility and creating life. I pitched my idea to the BBC and nine months later, my documentary *Fertility and Me* was broadcast.

It started a well-overdue conversation about a subject that, for some bizarre reason, is still taboo. It also highlighted the fact that there are tons of couples like you and me who are starting families in their thirties and forties for all sorts of reasons.

Joining the parenting club in our thirties and beyond means that we are spinning an extraordinary number of plates, often including a career that is at its peak. As a result, we are the first generation where our parenting roles aren't defined by gender. We are the first ones to mix it up and truly share the responsibility and joy of having a child. Today more than ever, both men and women are having conversations with their employers about flexible hours in the constant search for work/family-life balance, helped by the introduction in the UK of Shared Parental Leave in April 2015. Most of us co-parent or fly solo in the true sense of the word, relying solely on each other and/or friends when, more often than not, extended family are too far away to help on a regular basis. Our parents could look to their parents for guidance, but this situation is new, modern and unique. We can only look to our peers for guidance, support and empathy, which is why I wanted to include as many voices as possible in this book. Thanks to everyone who shared their stories with me. They made me laugh, cry and often made me challenge my own parenting skills.

We're rewriting the rulebook and winging it, but we are winging it together!

'I feel it's important women should be open and honest about childbirth and motherhood with zero judgement!' Sadie

'I do think being a slightly older first time Mum throws challenges out there for you but you know what, bring it on! Giving birth isn't a walk in the park so it doesn't mean being a parent will be either! But it's still the best job in the world!' Naomi

THE
TOP 5
MOST ANNOYING
THINGS

YOU MIGHT HEAR WHEN STARTING OUT*
*and must just ignore

1   Have you started trying yet?

2   Don't you think you're a bit... Old?

3   The clock's ticking you know...

4   Are you worried that you don't have enough energy to be a parent now?

5   You career-folk, always leaving it to the last minute

PREGNANT
BUT NOT PAST IT

I don't feel old, yet what was it that was written on my maternity notes? Oh yes, those delightful terms 'elderly primigravida' and 'geriatric mother'. I was 39 not 89, for goodness' sake. I have a feeling that it wasn't a woman who came up with these terms.

> 'I'll never forget the first time someone referred to me as a geriatric mother – I was 38, I couldn't believe it! It definitely took me a while to accept that I was going to be identified by my "advanced maternal age".' Jess

I googled other terms for 'older mother', looking for something softer, kinder, and found 'moth' and 'old goat'. Christ! Shouldn't the fact that we are now reproducing more than ever before past 35 be celebrated? But it's not – many maternity units genuinely make you feel like some sort of weird, rare species who against all odds has managed to conceive 'later in life' and should be handled with kid gloves. The reality is that **one in five births in the UK is now to a mother over the age of 35**. It may be time that the medical profession looked at changing the way they address us older mothers and find a way to stop making us feel quite so, well, OLD!

We are living longer than ever before; we are healthier than ever before and more active than ever before. Forty is definitely the new 30 and in some hospitals, they recognise that this term is less than flattering and have changed it to 'advanced maternal age'. It beats elderly, but it's still not great, is it?

However, primigravidas, the good news is that we are not the minority any more, absolutely not, because it is a fact that **more women are having babies over 40 than under 20 for the first time since the Second World War, and the over-35s have the fastest-growing birth rates in the last ten years.** Slowly but surely we are becoming the 'norm', especially if you live in a city. As an example, the youngest in our NCT group in West London was 34 and the eldest was 41.

Let's face it: older mothers get a tough time of it from the media. There is more good news: according to the *New York Times*, recent studies show that babies born to women between the ages of 35 and 39 performed better in cognitive tests compared to children who are born to mothers between 25 and 29 years of age. Also, when it comes to parenting attitudes and practice, a study led by Professor Tea Trillingsgaard from the University of Aarhus showed that older mothers are less likely to be harsh with their children, and the children themselves were less likely to have behavioural, social and emotional problems because the mothers have more psychological flexibility and more ability to tolerate whatever the children throw at them. Hmmm... I think this strongly depends on what kind of day you're having.

Being an older mum is nothing new though. Historically women would spread their births over many years and would sometimes be a grandmother by the time their youngest child was born. In the 1920s, the average age a woman would have her last child was 42.

While having a child later in life may not necessarily be a choice, the obvious upsides are that women post-35 are often better educated, more financially stable, confident and, going back to that study, far more patient, which, let's face it, is key! I am constantly surprised with how much patience I have with Teddy. It really was a failing of mine in the past, so much so that when we wrote our own wedding vows I made Charlie promise to take less time in the shower (25 minutes is ridiculous to be fair) and be a better timekeeper and he made me promise to embrace camping (yet to happen: cited pregnancy and early motherhood as solid reasons not to go for most of 2016 and all of 2017) and to develop more patience! It was an issue.

I know without a shadow of a doubt that I wouldn't have been the mother I am today 10 years ago. At 30, I was preoccupied with my career during the day and with socialising at night and, more importantly, I'd yet to meet the man who would become my teammate in the parenting game.

Medical research and media articles tend to focus negatively on age-related fertility risks, and the underlying message is that we must drop everything and have a baby. After making the documentary last year, I know that there is certainly a lot of truth to that, and in a perfect world that is what we should all do to maximise our chances, but if only life was that simple. It isn't necessarily the case that women 'put off' having a baby, but life circumstances will always dictate when is the right time to start a family.

'I was scared of being an "older" mum: the thought that I might be leaving my daughter before I had seen her through all of life's ups and downs; the thought of being judged as an "older" mum, and the media's perception that I had chosen to go after a career rather than have children. What actually was the case was that I wanted to be in a stable relationship, which didn't happen until later in my life.' Gemma

MY JOURNEY TO A BABY

At 32, I broke up with a nice boy who I'd shared a happy seven years with and, amid the panic that I was suddenly in my thirties and starting out again on the man front, I decided that while a big question mark hung over my personal life, I might as well focus on my career. In the year that followed, I landed my dream job and moved to London. My career was firing on all cylinders, but my personal life was a bit of a damp squib.

It took five years for Charlie and me to meet, start dating, fall in love, argue about whether we would stay in the UK or move to Charlie's beloved homeland of New Zealand, nearly break up over that same conversation ten times over, make up after all those times, buy a house, renovate a house, get engaged, get married and try for a baby.

'In the back of your mind you know that you're getting on a bit, but you're not exactly going to ask "will you have a baby with me?" on the first date!' Vikki

Five years would have been nothing had we been in our twenties, but we were in our mid-thirties, and while there was no denying that the dreaded tick-tock, tick-tock was nearly audible, I took my chance and didn't bow to the pressure, hoping that we would still be lucky down the line if we let everything play out in its own time. It was a gamble.

There is no denying that had I made the documentary about fertility sooner, and had a broader understanding of the subject it would have led me to push the issue a bit more and make decisions sooner. I still feel that men and women should be better educated about our fertility and the consequences of trying later in life, regardless of whether it be a choice or not. Forewarned is forearmed.

HOW OLD IS TOO OLD?

Safe sex was a very strong message at school and, of course, a very important one. Back then, the focus was on avoiding STDs and not getting pregnant but, let's face it, equally, we need to understand our limitations in terms of fertility. The crux of the matter is that while we are looking younger on the outside, our insides are biologically wired to reproduce before 45. Try as we might, there is no super smoothie or vitamin out there that can magically boost your egg supply. When they're gone, they're gone. Game over.

It's not exclusively a woman's issue either; men's sperm is on average 50 per cent less effective after the age of 40. Ah yes, we're not told that, are we? The common assumption is that men can go on having babies into their seventies, eighties even – and some do – but it's no good if they then can't pick the baby up, is it?

So, how old is too old to become a parent? There isn't of course a definitive answer; it's for everybody to take a long, hard and realistic look at their situation in order to decide. I met a woman during the making of the documentary who, thanks to a successful donor egg, had her much-longed-for child at 50.

Some may argue that 50 is too old, and I will admit that I had preconceived ideas. But meeting Sarah with her three-year-old son and hearing how she had battled for seven years before eventually giving birth to her little boy really touched me.

Yes, she loved her career, but it was filling a baby-shaped hole. At 43, she met her now husband on a plane and decided that she wanted to give motherhood her best shot. As she sat on the floor, building a train track with her boy, she exuded joy from every pore.

I wasn't pregnant at that point and had no idea how long it would take, or indeed whether we would experience as complicated a journey, but meeting Sarah helped me relax, knowing that however long it took, the outcome would be worth every second.

THE MATHS OF BEING OLDER

As I wrote this, I was away in Northern Ireland for *The One Show*. My boss is a big supporter of parents being able to bring their children to work, and that week he had his own son with him as it was school holidays and childcare was an issue. My boss, Sandy who's 57, had Raffe, his son, when he was 45. I'll do the maths for you: Raffe is now 12. As we travelled along in the car we had a long conversation about parenting later in life. My deputy editor, who had just had his second son at 47, was also keen to get involved in the conversation. Sandy is adamant that age really is just a number and pointed out that he is a lot more active with Raffe than many other dads in Raffe's class. They play sports together regularly and every morning on that trip to Northern Ireland, they went off to explore various coves and beaches on the coast, to climb, hire boats, or discover an exhibition together. The bond between them is undeniable and Raffe is in his element. I asked him what it's like to have an 'older' dad. He looked slightly perplexed, and with a shrug of the shoulders said, 'Dad is just Dad... he's awesome!' Great answer.

Mortality is something that constantly plays on my mind. Every day, without fail, I play the same game: when Teddy's 10, I'll be 49, when he's 20, I'll be 59, when he's 30, I'll be 69; when he's 60, I'll be – oh shit – 99, and probably not around. The outcome is never different however many times I say it. It sometimes freaks me out that Mam had her first child when she was nearly 15 years younger than I was when I fell pregnant with Teddy. She was 25 when I was born and Dad was 27, having met, married and got tied into a mortgage by the ages of 23 and 25 respectively. By the time I came along, they were fully grown, mature adults. What a difference a generation makes; I was still behaving like a teenager at their age.

I asked Mum about her experience of becoming a mother, and how she thought it compared to mine. Did she have more energy as a new mum at 25 than I did at 39? Did her and Dad find the first few months harder as they were younger with less life experience? We'd drunk a whole pot of tea between us before we reached the conclusion that while it was different, both situations presented equal numbers of positives and negatives.

She reasoned that no, they didn't have more energy, particularly as Dad, who was a newly qualified engineer on a low wage, was working all the hours God sent to provide for his new family, because Mum had decided to quit her cashier job at the bank to focus on being a mother, and didn't return to part-time work until I was five. She had no help as she had lost her own mother at 16 and was very much flying solo as soon as she left the hospital. As for experience, losing her mother at 16 had meant that Mum had had to learn to run a household and care for her younger brother while my grandfather was out earning a living, and these skills had come in handy when she had a family of her own. So, at 25, she was way more equipped experience-wise than I was at 39. While Charlie and I were financially more stable, we had no clue about what we were doing, but having looked after ourselves well, our energy levels matched those of a mid-twenties parent.

Grandparents

I still think of my parents as being young even though they're now in their mid- to late sixties. They've always been active, and continue to lead very active lives. They watch what they eat, well, Dad falls off the wagon sometimes and puts his whole head in the fridge so that he can gulp down large quantities of Cadbury's Whole Nut, but Mum is quick to pull him back into line. For this reason, touch wood, they can be hands-on grandparents to Teddy, and to Dash and Indiana, my sister's children. I know how lucky we are, because many of my friends' parents are suffering from ill health in their late sixties, early seventies and, try as they might, are unable to provide the level of support that they would like for their children.

However, it does leave me wondering whether Charlie and I will be able to offer the same support to Teddy when – and if – he decides to have children of his own. When Mum and Dad walked into the hospital room to visit Ted for the first time after he was born, one of the first things that struck me was that Charlie and I would be 78 and 79 if Teddy had his first child at the same age as us.

I have a very close relationship with my own grandmother, Teddy's great-grandmother, who absolutely adores him and will sing to him until the cows come home, but naturally, due to old age, is unable to look after him on her own or even pick him up when he's crying. I'm reminded on visits that I will be closer to her age should Ted decide to have children in his forties.

Ted and his great-grandmother

WE ARE WHERE WE ARE

The bigger picture is that the shape of society is changing before our very eyes. Many children born in Teddy's generation may go through life never experiencing having grandparents, which is a crying shame. Instead, though, children like Ted will have older parents who have waited longer for them for one reason or another, who will therefore really appreciate what a gift they are. That's not to say that younger parents don't appreciate their children too; it's more that when you're older, there's a fear that it will never happen to you, which isn't the case for a younger mum. I hope that we will recognise and remember how precious time is and prioritise spending it with him despite us having established careers. Every day will not be perfect, and mistakes will definitely be made and are being made daily, but our intention is always good. Children want nothing more than our time, and as much as we can, that is what we will give him.

Ted has changed our world exponentially for the better. There is some regret about not getting our act together sooner, but we are where we are, and we're very grateful for what we have. As they say, hindsight is a wonderful thing.

'The beginning of my story was the second chance at being in love with my perfect man, but as a result I was a little older and a little less predictable with my periods, meaning fertility was not a given. I had had scans and tests in the past, but when we decided that we would like to start a family it was a worry in my mind. However, as fate would have it this was not the case. I was suffering from severe abdominal pain and went to the on call GP service on 14 November... it was the best appendicitis I could have wished for as this was the day I discovered that I was pregnant. The doctor was crying with happiness alongside me... I couldn't believe how fortunate we were. And as for the long-term plan, we ended up having our 12 week scan instead of making a fertility appointment. The world of becoming pregnant is such a minefield; until you try you don't know if you can, but the later you leave it in life the more difficult it can be, but to have the right partner is so important. To finish off the perfect week of news, the Saturday of that same week my partner asked me to marry him ...we now have Isabelle, who is five months old and completely dreamy, and we are getting married on 16 December. If only life was like a book or film script when you know everything will be OK. Then all the time spent on worry and concern could be put to far better use.' Emma

PART
1

LIFE BEFORE

THE
TOP 5
MOST ANNOYING
THINGS

YOU MIGHT HEAR DURING PREGNANCY*
*and must just ignore

1 Congratulations! Was it planned?

2 I sailed through my pregnancy, I felt better than ever! Then again I was 27.

3 You look so tired – are you OK?

4 Is it twins?

5 My labour was practically orgasmic.

1+1=3: A CHANGE IS COMING

. . .

If you're expecting a baby, or indeed considering having a baby in the near future, take a long hard look at your life as it is right now. Go on, take a few minutes and really think about what it looks like this second because, as those of us who are already parents know, it will never be the same again.

People will tell you this over and over from the moment you fall pregnant, but you will simply not believe them. If you're anything like Charlie and me, you'll think that you'll be that couple who will travel with your baby, carry on going to restaurants, take him or her to festivals and not get obsessed with a routine.

There are some couples who absolutely manage all this and more... but they are in the minority – and brave!

The rest of us try to do all of the above and quickly realise that routine is your new best friend and that the last thing on earth you want to do is sit with a small, unpredictable baby in a restaurant or in any other situation that involves a public area.

Your world, for the first year, will shrink and you will spend more time in your own home than ever before. It's a mammoth shock to the system. It certainly takes a lot of adjustment, and some days the realisation that your old life has slipped away can be a bitter pill to swallow regardless of how longed-for your baby may be.

MANAGING EXPECTATIONS

Don't panic; it does get easier after the first intense six months and glimpses of your old life will appear, like rays of sunshine through dense clouds. The upside of being an older parent is that you've probably done restaurants, bars, cinemas, festivals and weekends away to death anyway.

I definitely felt ready for a gear change, a new rhythm. Still as frenetic and hectic as the old one, but in a different way. The good news is that your new life will probably be vastly more fulfilling than the old one, better in hundreds of ways that you just can't know about until you experience it for yourself. Don't panic, because the change is gradual. Your old couple life (or lifestyle if you're on your own) will start to morph into something brand-new the second you realise you want a baby.

We were delighted when I fell pregnant with Ted, but, like everybody else, we never really considered the monumental impact he would have on our lives. During my pregnancy we mostly focused on the birth. That was the first mistake. Of course, the birth is a big deal, which we'll talk about in detail later (brace yourselves) but in hindsight it's sort of the straightforward part, in as much as it will just happen. You will be with experts who will know what they're doing and they will guide you through it. It will be painful, but it's sort of out of your control.

Naively, I never seriously considered what would happen past that point, or maybe I did and just pictured myself hand in hand with Charlie, Ted strapped into a Baby Bjorn, as we enjoyed long walks at the weekend. It turns out there's definitely more to it than that.

There are *some* idyllic hours that are nearly what you imagined all those months ago as you patted your bump, but most of the time, it's Bedlam (in the best possible way!). So, let's tackle it stage by stage and start at the very beginning.

'I absolutely loved being pregnant! I had a stress-free pregnancy, in fact I felt the healthiest I've ever felt! All was going great up until I was 37 weeks and slipped on some mud and broke my elbow in two places! After hours of tears, regular checks on baby by midwives and all of the surgeons, anaesthetists and other important people involved in trying to figure what was best for me and the baby I was finally booked in to have surgery the following day. Being nil by mouth for a heavily pregnant woman is torture! Before being wheeled away into surgery I heard a midwife say to a doctor "keep checking under that blanket, that baby's going to come I think." Petrified, anxious and hungry, I said bye to my husband not sure that by the time I woke up I might be a mum. Four and a half hours of surgery later I woke up craving a can of Coke and with a comfortable little baby still safe and sound in my bump. I went home the next day and set up camp downstairs on the sofa, which was my base for a week as I wasn't able to go upstairs by myself. I started physio straight away to try and build up as much strength as possible in preparation for looking after a newborn. Twenty-six days after my fall my baby girl, Posie, was born after much persuasion by me to the midwife to allow me to have a water birth (they were concerned in case they needed to get me out of the pool quickly and hurt my arm. I assured them that my husband could chuck me out quickly if need be! Luckily this didn't happen!) So, 21 months later I have one titanium plate, eight pins, a whopping scar and a beautiful toddler.' Charlotte

LET'S GET IT ON...

Tiredness, headaches, cramping, sore boobs, constipation... I found myself constantly googling signs of early pregnancy even though I absolutely knew what the classic symptoms were. As soon as we got married, I ditched the contraceptive pill and quietly focused on getting pregnant.

At 18, I would have imagined that by 25 I'd be married with our first baby imminent, but it turns out that I was more than a decade out. At 32 and single, I landed my job on *The One Show* and moved to London. It was brand-new and all-consuming. It was and still is my dream job so I needed to focus hard and pull out all the stops to prove that I deserved to sit on that green sofa on BBC One's flagship show. That took every ounce of confidence that I had, which meant that there was none left in the first months of my new job for handsome men.

Some people make the mistake of assuming that men and women with successful careers in their mid-thirties must have decided somewhere down the line to concentrate on furthering themselves in the workplace as opposed to starting a family, and it's true in some cases, but not in all. Having a family isn't everybody's cup of tea and that's fine. But for the rest of us, work is a distraction. We haven't purposely found ourselves in jobs that are demanding of our time and energy so that we can avoid having babies. No! We are making the most of opportunities that present themselves because there is no guarantee that having a family will be one of them. We don't end up desperate for a baby at 40 because it's only just occurred to us that it might be a 'nice thing to do'. In most cases, we are where we are.

There is one option that is available to us all, an insurance without a guaranteed payout, and that's egg freezing. It's a big investment, with the costs of treatments ranging between £3,000 and £5,000, but success rates, even with the latest vitrification technology, are still disappointing. It wasn't something I thought about or knew anything about in my early thirties and, even if I had, I probably wouldn't have considered it, naively assuming that my fertility was bulletproof, but 37-year-old Zoe Williams made a film on the very subject for *The One Show* and as a result is considering treatment.

'I always knew I wanted a family and planned to start trying from the age of 32, but at 32 I found myself single and now at 37 I'm still not in a relationship where starting a family is an option. So I'm freezing my eggs, in the hope that this could increase my chances in the future when the time is right... If you're 30+, sure that you want children and in a financial position to consider egg freezing, then it's worth starting doing your research; I would also recommend having initial fertility tests with counselling though, prior to spending large amounts of money on something that is not a guarantee.' Dr Zoe Williams, NHS GP and media medic for ITV's *This Morning* and BBC2's *Trust Me, I'm A Doctor*

Some of the biggest companies like Apple and Facebook are spending tens of thousands on freezing their female colleagues' eggs for them. Yes, it's one of the perks of working for one of the big players. The idea is that female employees will have more freedom when planning their families and it lets them delay having children while progressing their career. This may be appealing for some young women but critics say that this policy sends out the message that work is more important than family, and that a woman can't have both at the same time. While I'm completely on board with the idea that egg freezing certainly boosts a woman's chances of conceiving later, it's a shame that big corporations can't also work harder at creating an environment that's conducive and welcoming for working parents. Embracing the idea that women *and* men can work and have a family, side by side with the offer of egg freezing if wanted, would be the healthiest way forward, it seems to me.

Meeting my teammate

In March 2011, both of us dressed as cowboys, I met my husband-to-be at a fancy-dress house party; I was 33, and he was 32.

When we first locked eyes, he was holding court in the middle of the kitchen dressed in a knitted, Mexican-style poncho. Fetching. We chatted about nothing in particular, but through the haze of lukewarm cheap wine, a spark flew. The next time I saw him was about a month later at a mutual friend's birthday. It was a Sunday lunchtime affair, and Charlie arrived hungover. He had slept at his best friend Trevor's house the night before and had borrowed some of his clothes to come to the lunch. I only need to tell you that while Charlie stands at six foot two, Trevor is about five foot eight, for you to get a picture of the shambles of an outfit that Charlie was wearing: a faded rock T-shirt that would have been a duster in my house and jeans that skimmed his ankles. Despite his sartorial misgivings, after chatting non-stop during the lunch I found myself drawn to this laid-back Kiwi with a big appetite for life and, more importantly, big bushy eyebrows.

He called three days later and left a voicemail. My heart was pounding. 'Hi Alex, it's Charles.' He sounded very formal, probably a throwback to his English parents who, despite having emigrated to Auckland 40 years ago, still sound like the Queen and Prince Philip. He wanted to take me out, he said, and I was impressed by the old-fashioned approach, no cryptic text, just a straightforward voice message. We arranged to meet at a pub that is literally at the end of the street where we live now. We had our first date there and have celebrated every other milestone at the same table ever since.

Deep down, I'm a bit of a traditionalist (don't judge me) and wanted to get married before we had children. Our biggest regret is not getting married sooner, especially now that we have Teddy. There were two contributing factors as to why we waited. Firstly, Charlie is extremely indecisive and he had to come to terms with the fact that if he was to marry me, his life would then be in the UK, as opposed to his beloved Auckland, and secondly, we were blasé when it came to fertility and just assumed that we wouldn't have a problem. We were busy enjoying each other, treating ourselves to fancy holidays and restaurants after stressful periods of work. It never occurred to us that if we wanted to have children we should bloody well get on with it.

By the time we got to our late thirties, conversations with friends had become more and more centred on how so and so were still trying for a baby after three years and how so and so had started their first cycle of IVF. Out of nowhere, bam, it was on our radar.

PURDEY & MADELINE

Maddie and I have always wanted to have a family and experience pregnancy. Being in a same-sex relationship never changed this desire but it posed some obvious challenges! However, seven years after starting our journey to make our family, we are lucky enough to have two happy and healthy boys: Tayt, aged five, and Gray, one.

When we decided to have a family, we looked into the options available to us, including IVF. We ended up opting for 'intra-partner donation' – basically becoming each other's egg donors and the closest way we could get to making a baby together. One of us would have her eggs harvested, fertilised and then an embryo would be implanted into the other. With the help of an anonymous donor – who we chose for his similar interests and characteristics to us – we would both be involved in the process. Our intention was that we would both get to carry.

We are in a unique position as both of us have been on both sides of a pregnancy. This was definitely an advantage as we could empathise with each other, be it over the side effects of the drugs, the experiences of miscarriage or the immense joy of feeling the baby move for the first time or of course, giving birth.

We chose an anonymous donor from overseas because we were not looking for someone to be part of our family. We are so grateful that people donate to help those of us who cannot conceive naturally. Both our boys have the same male donor so they are half-siblings genetically, as well as being brothers, of course.

We make sure our boys have strong, positive male role models in their lives. We are also very open about our journey to becoming parents in the hope that it helps same-sex female couples see what options are available to them. In turn, we hope that sharing our story will make families like ours more and more common in the future.

Maddie and I went through eight rounds of IVF in total to get our two boys, all self-funded. We both had fertility problems, which were not picked up in the initial fertility tests, and this certainly added to the number of cycles we had to have. Maddie has PCOS, which resulted in her overstimulating when egg harvesting – she ended up in hospital twice due to this. I had a high level of natural killer cells, which meant my body would see an embryo as something to be fought off, so I would typically miscarry around six or seven weeks. We tried to remain optimistic, as with each failed attempt the medical team learnt more about us and would adjust things for the next cycle, giving us hope that the next time would work. In the end, we both carried to full term on our fourth attempt.

It was very hard at times to find the strength, physically, mentally and emotionally, to try again and again, but, like so many people, we did. We'd advise to get as many tests as possible done before starting IVF – the more that is known about both parties the better. This is even more relevant for same-sex couples who cannot try to conceive naturally.

Neither of us feel any differently towards either of our boys. I carried Tayt, but I have no genetic link to him as he is made from Maddie's egg and donor sperm. Maddie carried Gray, who comes from my egg and the same donor sperm. We could not love either of our children any more. However, in both of our experiences, there is a different bond between the mother and child carried. We both feel more responsible for the child we carried and we both have the ability to read his needs a bit easier than the one we didn't. We don't think this is surprising, as the experience of carrying, giving birth and then nursing a baby is so intimate.

It's amazing what IVF has allowed us to do. We feel truly blessed to have two healthy boys and that we both had the opportunity to carry one. We are so grateful to all the doctors, nurses and embryologists who have made our family possible. Now if they could just get rid of our eye bags everything would be perfect!

Getting a move on

After we got married I replaced the Pill with a daily sludgy smoothie (I never got the consistency right, and it was often like drinking a gritty puddle), full to the brim with anything that I had read was good for fertility. Spinach, flaxseed, matcha powder, berries and lots of walnuts, which Charlie often gets a bit of a reaction to, nothing serious, just a swollen tongue, so I didn't tell him. I worried about sex becoming functional so I decided to wait three months before introducing ovulation sticks and there were definitely no graphs tracking my temperature, but I did everything possible to boost our chances. I had always exercised moderately but my regime was stepped up a gear, alcohol was consigned to weekends only (that was very hard to begin with) and sex was very much on the agenda. I know people out there say that every three to five days is sufficient, but well, why take the risk? We attacked it with gusto, while keeping things 'light' and 'fun'. At the same time I was making the documentary for BBC1, and what I discovered during those months of filming intrigued and scared me in equal measure. In a lab in a posh fertility clinic in Central London, I watched fascinated as the professor showed me how an Intracytoplasmic Sperm Injection, more commonly referred to as ICSI, works. I looked on in wonder as the chosen sperm was inserted under a microscope into an egg from a 36-year-old woman, two years younger than me at the time. The professor carefully used the end of the pipette to try to pierce the 'zona pellucida', or egg wall, in order to introduce the sperm. He very gently made contact with the wall and the entire egg crumbled. The egg was old, tired and useless. In that moment, I understood how age affects fertility and it became very real. That, without a doubt, was the strongest and most emotive image of the entire documentary for me. I was petrified as I waited for the results of my fertility test that I had agreed to have done as part of the documentary.

Test yourself

Up until this point I had never considered that I should, or even could, have a test to check how fertile I was. If you are struggling to conceive, ask your GP who can arrange some investigations (if appropriate) – knowledge is power. The first test that the doctor will do is a simple blood test that will check your hormone levels for progesterone to see whether you're ovulating. You can also ask for a transvaginal ultrasound scan that will check the health of your womb, ovaries and for any blockages in your Fallopian tubes that might have been caused by endometriosis or fibroids. These are good tests to knock off to give you a fuller picture of where you are fertility-wise.

The more I learnt about how age and a stressful lifestyle can impact on your chances of conceiving, the more I worried about the test results, coupled with the fact that in the process of making the documentary, I had also found out that Mum had gone through the menopause at 43. Forty-three! That was a huge bombshell. Mum, in her typical no-nonsense way, had casually slipped it into the conversation while cutting a piece of Victoria sponge in my sister's kitchen. To put this into context, that is the same age as Kate Beckinsale, Tyra Banks and Victoria Beckham. You don't imagine them with night sweats and on HRT, do you? When menopause strikes, it really is game over, and if I followed in my mum's footsteps, I was just five years away from that event. That was the really big wake-up call to get on it.

Male fertility

We also talked about male fertility as part of the documentary and I spent a considerable amount of time talking about sperm with one of the leading specialists on male fertility in the UK, a lovely bloke called Professor Allan Pacey. This was his bombshell... A male's fertility will *halve* after the age of 40! What?! I mean weren't we all under the impression that men could continue to procreate for as long as they could be bothered to have sex? Well, apparently not, and this was straight from the guy who knew everything there was to know about penises and sperm. All this time, women had been led to believe that we were the only ones who had a fertility window before we became all dried up on the egg front, but it turns out that that is a problem that both genders very much share. There's some tips from him at the end of the chapter.

THE DAY OF RECKONING

I was anxious the day of my test results, and with sweaty palms I walked towards the consultant's room, sorry now that I had agreed to take the test on camera. It felt too personal and too big to share. Charlie was also worried. He didn't feel that I'd considered the magnitude of the news that I was about to receive when I agreed to the test. He was right. The next half an hour would dictate the shape of our future. Considering my age, there was a high possibility that it wouldn't be great news. I had been on the Pill for years and had no idea how fertile I was. The considerate consultant gave me a warm smile as I entered the room, easing my nerves immediately. Thankfully, it was good news: I wasn't super-fertile, but my egg reserve was pretty good for 38 and I had no signs of endometriosis, polycystic ovaries or anything else that might be problematic.

The relief I felt to hear that things were OK and as they should be was huge. I have every sympathy for all those couples who don't get the news they want. I can't pretend to know how it would feel to realise that you have a fertility battle of any kind on your hands.

My doctor was incredibly helpful when I broached the subject of conceiving. She was informed and presented me with a lot of tips and advice, including having the fertility test as soon as possible. However, too many friends have complained how their doctors have unhelpfully just told them to keep trying and to come back in a year. Such ignorance could really cost someone their chance of having a family. Insist on these tests that I've mentioned and give yourself a fair chance.

> 'After years of trying, a miscarriage and two failed NHS-funded IVF cycles, during which I lost my mum and stepdad, we decided to go travelling for a year. When we came home we gave IVF one more go and went to a clinic in the Czech Republic. We got the long-awaited positive test, and then at the 12-week scan we were told that we were having triplets!' Kelly

I fell pregnant in April, just two months after I'd stopped taking the Pill. Charlie may have had a swollen tongue thanks to the walnuts, but my goodness, they had worked. Our mission was accomplished, and far quicker than we expected, and we were ecstatic. It could have been a fluke but I hope that it will give some of you peace of mind that just because we're having babies older doesn't necessarily mean that fertility struggles are inevitable. It's not always age-specific: let's not forget that mothers who are a decade and more younger can experience a complicated fertility journey too.

Lorna

I am a mummy to triplets; I have severe PCOS and struggled to get pregnant for over 18 months, but finally became a mummy at 37. My story is a bittersweet one, as one of my daughters, Essie, suffered a catastrophic brain injury at birth. We lost her last year, but I have chosen to embrace the life we've been given and use Essie's story to help others. Plus I have to be strong, because simply I have no choice, as I am a mummy and you find a strength and purpose that you didn't think was possible.

PROFESSOR ALLAN PACEY
Professor of Andrology
and Reproductive Medicine

There is a lot that males can do to help with their reproductive health; I recommend focusing on the following five things:

DON'T SMOKE
Smoking can increase the genetic damage to sperm.

WEAR LOOSE UNDERWEAR
Tight underwear can lower the number of swimming sperm a man produces.

EAT HEALTHILY

Men who have a high level of fruit and vegetables in their diet generally have better sperm.

HAVE REGULAR SEX

No need to save up sperm, just keep a supply of fresh sperm coming through by having regular sex.

START AS EARLY AS YOU CAN

The sperm from older men above 40 is generally not as good as that from younger men.

'All my friends were getting pregnant, and I wasn't – I felt like such a failure. Of course you're over the moon for our friends, but it does shine a light on your own situation; I didn't feel like I could talk to them about it either because we were in such different places, and I didn't want to bring them down either. It was a lonely place to be. We couldn't believe when the IVF worked first time – we were *overjoyed*.' Vikki

ZITA WEST
Fertility Expert

One of the commonest questions I get asked is, '*I want to know about my fertility status and how long I have got*'.

Different women have different challenges when it comes to thinking about planning to have a baby.

These questions are difficult to answer, as fertility isn't black and white: there are so many shades of grey. The simple fact is that some women are luckier than others and have better egg reserves.

In helping women with their fertility, I spend a lot of time trying to make them aware of the possible delays in the process and the consequences of delay, and how they need to be strategic in their decisions. This I understand is difficult, because everybody's situation is different: there are issues of timing, finances, work, feeling ready, not having met a man, just having come out of a relationship, etc.

On average it takes eight to 12 months to get pregnant, and of course longer for some women, and it's also very common to miscarry, which can delay further. You will need to try again, so more months pass. When you do get pregnant, you have the nine-month pregnancy plus time to recover after the birth, so 18 months can easily go by. Most women I see want more than one child, so you need to plan ahead and often don't have time to waste. A lot of women don't appreciate this.

Couples increasingly want to do all they can to help themselves. They want to feel proactive. The hardest factor they have to deal with is uncertainty: not knowing when and how. Managing their expectations is something I do daily.

Certainly, lifestyle stresses like work-life balance play their role, but there is also the underlying mindset.

Women are great at managing so many aspects of their lives, until it comes to fertility. It is easy to feel the pressure very early on when it hasn't happened. After a couple of months, not being pregnant can take you over: you can become obsessed about measurements, timings and gadgets, especially around ovulation. It can affect relationships badly: I see men on a daily basis with nothing wrong with them other than they can't perform because they feel under pressure to do so.

Throw your temperature charts away if you have been doing them for a long time. Take the pressure off one another. Remember, too, that sperm will survive in you for three to five days, so there is no need to time everything around the moment of ovulation. If you have sex three times a week, you can be confident that sperm will be available when you ovulate: focus on the sperm, not the egg.

Sarah

I'd known my partner for six months before we found out that he had cancer. We knew we wanted a family together so after multiple consultations, we made the decision to freeze his sperm. After trying (and not succeeding) we found out that I had cysts. Five rounds of IVF later, and I'm due to give birth to our first child at the age of 42. Needless to say, this wasn't exactly the plan – but it is what it is, and the most important thing is that we are about to be parents, and we could not be more thrilled.

9 MONTHS 'TIL LIFT OFF

The familiar *One Show* theme tune belted out over the studio floor. Emily, one of our floor managers, was counting us to on air, backwards from ten. I sat there, furiously rubbing marks on my shoulders where my bra was digging in, and then remembered that the top button on my jeans was also undone, too late... 'Welcome to *The One Show*.' We were on air. I had been breathing in for the last 19 weeks, hoping that nobody would notice my growing baby bump, but tonight was the night when the cat would be let out of the bag. Up until now, I had only told family and very close friends, along with my boss and a few other colleagues on a 'need-to-know' basis.

The thing is that it's practically impossible to hide your pregnancy if you're in a relationship and of a certain age. I had been married four months and I was 39 years old. From the minute I got back from honeymoon, viewers were on 'baby watch'. Even an unflattering trouser could work some people into a pregnancy frenzy! Most of these people in question were also women who had children, and I was constantly surprised that none of them seemed to understand the reasons why I might not want to announce the pregnancy before we'd had the 20-week scan and were reassured that all was well.

Pop star Cheryl was pregnant at the same time and we were criticised heavily when she was a guest on *The One Show* for not asking her if she was pregnant. As someone who was in the same position, I absolutely knew that she was pregnant and as she commented on my bump we shared a little knowing smile, but I still refused to ask her outright. It was her choice to keep it a secret and she was absolutely entitled to her privacy. She would have had her reasons for not wanting to announce her pregnancy, and that was that.

While every woman's pregnancy will be unique, the constant bewilderment is very much a shared experience, so I'll talk you through mine – highs, lows and everything in between – in the hope that some of your questions may be answered along the way.

TWO PINK LINES

Let's start at the very beginning. It was the first balmy evening of the year, unseasonably hot for the end of April, and we were sat in the local beer garden after work, the cold wine slipping down a treat. It was a Thursday so nothing heavy, just a couple of glasses to wash away the stresses of the day. At closing time, we said goodnight to our neighbours, and as I stood, the alcohol suddenly took hold and with a noisy thud I found myself on my back, unattractively wedged between the picnic bench and the small wall that protected the shrubbery behind us. I still have the scar. I was drunk. That horrible, room-spinning sort of drunk.

The next morning, I felt dreadful, like I'd drunk a whole bottle of port, not two glasses of wine. I'm one of those annoying people who rarely get hangovers, so this didn't make sense. I staggered through the day, heavy-headed, nauseous and baffled by the events of the night before. In hindsight, it was obvious. I was pregnant.

There were other clues. Friends came to stay and where I'd usually still be howling untunefully to Adele at 3am, steadfast in my 'one for the road' attitude, alcohol was the last thing I wanted and bed was number one on the priority list. I was already a changed woman.

Even so, I didn't twig for a very long time. I had recently come off the Pill and my cycle was all over the place and I suppose I didn't dare hope that we could be expecting so soon.

A close friend was also trying to get pregnant at the same time and, unlike me, she was obsessed with ovulation sticks. Her cycle had a bounty on its head and she was tracking it within an inch of its life. I have no idea of how many kits she had in the cupboard, but she filled a Sainsbury's bag for life for me and said, 'Here, have a few.'

I'm a big believer in letting fate play its part, so I wanted us to let things happen naturally, for a few months at least, but curiosity got the better of me, and as soon as I got home, I was in the bathroom, trying to prise the cellophane off the box. Within a millisecond of doing the test, a very prominent line appeared in the window. It was significantly quick and the line oddly dark. I stared at it for a long time, processing my thoughts. I grabbed my phone and started googling... can an ovulation test detect early pregnancy? It turns out that it can. The hormone that both the ovulation and pregnancy test are looking for is nearly identical in its make-up and so a standard ovulation kit is unable to distinguish between both, meaning that enough of either LH (which is the hormone that precedes ovulation) or hCG (which signals pregnancy) will give you a positive result.

My gut instinct told me that it would be too big a coincidence that I was at my most fertile on that particular day, especially considering my periods were so irregular. I knew in my heart of hearts that by some miracle we wouldn't be needing any more ovulation kits anytime soon.

The next morning, I bit the bullet and bought a pregnancy test. There I was, about to go for a run, casually sitting on the side of the bath in my gym gear, waving the pee-drenched stick in the air. My phone started ringing in the lounge and so I hurriedly chucked the test on the shelf above the sink and went off in search of my mobile. The phone rang off by the time I found it and I'd managed to listen to the voicemail, and email the person back, before remembering to go back to the test in the bathroom. In those five minutes, my life changed forever.

Even from the door of the bathroom I could see a very prominent line in the box. I stood still, staring at the piece of plastic that suddenly held so much importance. I was glued to the spot, blinking in disbelief. I then re-read the instructions in the box just to make sure that I'd properly understood what was what. It was positive. No doubt about it. We were having a baby. I needed to tell Charlie.

Without a moment's hesitation, I dialled his office landline.

'Hello, Charles Thomson.'

'Hi, we're having a baby!'

I'd blurted out the news just like that, without giving any consideration to the fact that my poor husband was sat in an open-plan office and really not expecting news of this magnitude.

There was a pause, and then a very measured and hushed, 'Well, that's great news, Al. I'm going to have to call you back.'

Not quite the reaction I had hoped for.

Three minutes later, my phone rang. Charlie had made it out of the office to somewhere more private and was shouting joyously down the phone, 'That's bloody great news, Al! We're gonna have a baby!'

'Yep, ten months of pregnancy, and then we'll be parents!'

Pause. 'Ten months?' Charlie blurted out, utterly bewildered. 'What do you mean, ten months?'

So here's the first thing you should know if you don't already. It takes 40–42 weeks in total to grow a baby. The common consensus may be that pregnancy is a nine-month affair, but it is in fact closer to ten.

In those ten months, you will be freaked out and blown away in equal proportion by what is happening to your body. It's marvellous and mind boggling all at once. Sometimes you will feel on top of the world both physically and mentally, and at other times overwhelmed, huge and potentially pretty unwell.

It's nothing to do with being in your late thirties or early forties though. Age has no great bearing on how a woman carries a baby. It's a fact that it's the age of a woman's eggs that limits her fertility, yet the uterus remains largely unaffected by the passage of years.

THE FIRST TRIMESTER

The first trip to the GP was a shock – I told her I was pregnant and she just took my word for it. I was prepared to be handed a sample bottle so that she could check for herself, but no, she just made a few notes, checked my blood pressure and asked me which hospital I wanted to be referred to. 'Hospital?' I asked blankly. She stopped typing and looked at me squarely. 'Yes, Charlotte (my first name and one nobody ever uses), you will need to decide where you want to have your baby as you will have all your scans and other pre-natal appointments there.'

I hadn't even thought about it. She gave me three choices of hospitals within my catchment area and I blindly picked the Queen Charlotte hospital based on the fact that it was the closest and, my namesake. Don't judge me. **If you're of a picky disposition, know that this question is coming and do some research before your first GP appointment.**

The initial excitement very quickly gave way to extreme exhaustion as classic first-trimester symptoms took hold. In terms of making a baby, the really big developmental stuff happens in the first trimester and that is why most of us feel pretty rubbish for those first 12 weeks in one way or another. I never suffered from morning sickness, thank goodness, but the tiredness that engulfed me between weeks six and 14 of my pregnancy was debilitating, full-on, narcolepsy-like episodes.

Tired... so tired

I'd wake up groggily, then promptly fall back asleep in the taxi on the way to work, then I'd struggle to keep my eyes open in our daily production meeting, often having to excuse myself to splash water on my face halfway through. Mid-afternoon, I'd gratefully retreat to the privacy of my dressing room to do some 'research', but really, I'd switch the lights off, curl up on the sofa under my coat and fall into a deep sleep. In the make-up chair an hour later, my eyes would feel horribly heavy and I'd struggle to prise them open between the light tickling of the make-up brushes as the girls blended my eyeshadow. I'd sometimes have to lie about a 'late night' and give in to the exhaustion, dribble running attractively down my chin. The adrenalin of live television just about kept me awake for rehearsal and the live broadcast and then I'd be asleep again in the taxi on the way home. I'd make it through supper, talking mostly about how tired I'd felt all day, and then crawl into bed at 10pm, wiped out. It was like this every day for eight weeks. The only thing that helped was carbohydrate, in big, scary quantities. Try as I might to fight it, salads really lost their shine and were replaced with sandwiches, and pasta became a firm favourite along with mash, chips, crisps, biscuits. I was like a Channel 4 documentary: *Bingeing on Beige Food*.

My friends, especially those who were already mothers, eyed me suspiciously but, knowing how precarious those first 12 weeks can be, were too polite to speculate. It's very hard not to have your cover blown in the early stages. As seismic changes are happening inside your body, on the outside you have to keep up a nigh-impossible pretence that nothing's different. It's tough. Never will you lie as blatantly to those closest to you. Typical excuses involving antibiotics for tooth infections will come spilling out, and good friends will nod sympathetically, fully aware of the subtext. Others, however, will clumsily dive in, head first, and ask you straight out, with a smug expression on their faces, whether you are indeed pregnant, leaving you floundering for an answer. These people are idiots and should be avoided at all costs.

The first trimester for me seemed the longest, and was definitely the hardest. I was emotional, unpredictable and, to be fair on Charlie, pretty tricky to live with. Everything was a worry and a stress when I should have been jumping for joy. A lot of that was the paranoia that came with falling pregnant at 39. I kept finding articles about the dangers of carrying a child in later life, laden with terrifying sweeping statements.

The risks of pregnancy later in life

It is true, of course, that as a woman gets older, both mother and baby face an increased risk of pregnancy complications, which include problems at delivery, high blood pressure during the course of the pregnancy, an increased chance of having a baby with congenital abnormalities such as Down's syndrome and an increased risk of miscarriage. It's a long list, but let's not forget that these risks are not exclusive to the over-35s, and most women in their thirties and forties have very healthy and uncomplicated pregnancies.

Despite being as healthy as I could and taking all the suggested supplements like folic acid (before and during pregnancy) and vitamins D, C and omega-3, I was paranoid that I would miscarry, especially as I had some spotting in the first eight to 10 weeks. I called the GP immediately and was assured that light spotting is normal in early pregnancy, that it happens to 20 per cent of women and is no cause for concern in most cases, but nothing could ease my mind. I'd seen too many friends go through the trauma and heartbreak of miscarriage and knew how cruelly common it was.

> 'I have had gestational diabetes this time round from seven weeks pregnant and I've ended up on metformin and insulin as well as sticking to a very strict diet. It's been tough thinking constantly about what you can eat, when you should eat, regular hospital appointments, managing hypos where your sugars crash and constant finger pricking and injections. I don't fit the stereotype of what people think a GD mum might look like, I was a normal weight when I got pregnant, was active and had no health issues.... I never believed I would have GD and just went through the motions of being tested. It also seems like a progressive condition that worsens with each pregnancy. Second time around has been so much worse and has seen me attend many more appointments and end up taking a lot of medication. Diet advice is also conflicting, with the NHS advocating a similar diet to those with type 2 but in actual fact many GD mums find this diet almost impossible to follow, causing blood sugars to rocket. It's such a difficult time being pregnant but then to find out you have a condition like GD, which is often beyond your control, adds to the stress. And I still find it crazy that as soon as your baby is born the condition is born!'
> Sarah

The first scan

The first scan is undoubtedly the most exciting part of the pregnancy. That first glimpse of our little foetus on the screen was singularly the best moment of our lives up until that point. Seeing that image appear took my breath away and almost three months of worry disappeared as we listened, delighted, to our baby's heartbeat for the first time. That scan was a game changer: from that point on, everything was different; I could now relax a little and start to enjoy the pregnancy.

As Charlie and I drove to the Queen Charlotte hospital that Friday morning, I remember being convinced that there wouldn't be an actual baby. I know that this sounds utterly ridiculous, but I'm sure it's a feeling that most first-time mothers experience. I was pretty tense as I lay on the bed while the sonographer rubbed the cold gel over my tummy. *Please let there be a baby in there.* We were completely silent, holding our breath until suddenly the ultrasound screen showed the image of a tiny little baby. Our relief, excitement and utter wonder was audible. We watched in fascination as each part of his little body was zoomed in on the screen.

'Oh look... there are the little hands and fingers!' Charlie exclaimed.

'Oh no,' answered the sonographer. 'There won't be fingers yet.'

'Right, so what are those five little digits then?' asked Charlie.

The sonographer, who looked about 12, wrinkled her nose and peered closely at the screen. 'Ah, yes... They're probably fingers.'

I'm glad she knew what she was doing.

Love and the urge to protect this little 12-week-old embryo hit us like a bolt out of the blue. I suppose that it's the very beginning of a bond like no other that will continue to grow and strengthen from that moment and last forever.

> 'I'd heard everyone always saying, "you just can't even imagine how much love you feel", but it really, properly shocked me at the first scan – I was bowled over by it.' David

We were skipping leaving the hospital, well, not literally as we would look insane, but you get the picture. We clutched our first pictures of our child, desperate to share our news. That evening, my parents were coming to London and so we casually suggested Skyping Charlie's parents in Auckland. After a few minutes' chat, we said that we had something to show the four of them and brought out the photo of the scan. The reaction was gold. A chorus of happy sobs erupted and I'll never forget my mother's words: 'Alun, our baby is having a baby.' Which is sort of stating the obvious, but I knew what she meant.

Wine was quickly replaced by champagne and even Charlie's parents got through a whole bottle at their end even though it was only 8.30 in the morning in the southern hemisphere!

THE SECOND TRIMESTER — AND BEYOND

As I moved into the second trimester the exhaustion dissipated and my usual energy levels were restored. I could exercise again, and although I tailored my regime to accommodate my bump, I felt as fit as I had done before I had a baby on board. Thankfully, my appetite also returned to normal, with green stuff back on the menu.

Nothing really happened between weeks 12 and 20. It was that in-between bit where I didn't have a bump but neither did I have any sort of waist. On the way to the bathroom one morning, I stood in the hall in front of the mirror in just my bra and knickers, and realised that I had become rectangular. Nothing went in any more; I was straight down on both sides. I looked like I'd gained a stone and a half, nothing drastic, but enough to make me doughy. I turned to the side, looking for a hint of a bump, but nothing, just bloat. I tried to breathe in. I couldn't do that either. I was stuck in no-man's-land.

The key event for me during those early weeks of the second trimester was meeting the midwife who would look after me for the rest of my pregnancy. She was called Lisa, a tanned, bike-riding fifty-something with a relaxed attitude and a good sense of humour. She was always available for a chat, offering me her mobile number at the first meeting, and answered any questions straightforwardly. Even when we talked about the birth, she encouraged me to try to do it as naturally as possible but she was also very honest about how painful it might be. There was never any pressure, even when I half-joked about wanting a C-section in the early days, naively thinking that that was an easier option. She presented all sides of every argument, allowing me to make informed choices. She managed my expectations, was as flexible as possible when it came to booking appointments and forgave me when I forgot my notes, which was practically every time!

My only disappointment was realising that Lisa wouldn't be present during the actual birth. I'd read that '**continuity of care**', which, as the name suggests, means that you have the same midwife from start to finish, often helps to ensure a better birth. I looked into it and found that having the same midwife is rare these days, and only booking a home birth would potentially allow for that to happen. As it turned out, I had fantastic labour midwives too and with Lisa top and tailing with antenatal and post-natal care, I felt very well cared for; but I can understand how a lack of continuity can cause immense anxiety. Talk to your midwife right at the beginning to ensure that you have a very clear picture of what sort of care is available to you.

Apart from close family and friends, we kept the news to ourselves, and up until week 18 I had more or less got away with people not asking too many questions. I had just continued to stuff myself into my jeans and wear slightly longer tops so that I could leave the top button open. I never really embraced maternity wear, mostly because I couldn't find stuff that I really liked, but by week 19, all my usual clothes were tight with a capital T and I would have to peel clothes off in my dressing room at the end of a show, my belly covered in unsightly red marks. My boobs nearly made their own escape plan on air once – all I did was breathe and three buttons across my chest came undone. It was time to give in and come clean.

I was desperate to wait until the 20-week scan before telling the world and its wife that we were pregnant, just so that we had as much peace of mind as possible, but we couldn't wait a minute longer before people would have just started assuming, so we made an appointment for an early scan at 19 weeks. **If you ever find yourself wanting to book a private scan, always shop around and compare prices.** I had five quotes in total, the highest being £500. We ended up paying £95, so obviously prices vary hugely.

On the drive to the clinic we'd been debating whether we wanted to find out the sex of our baby. We discussed all the pros and cons and still couldn't reach a decision. We wanted a surprise, but would knowing help us bond more with the child? Around and around we went and the conversation continued even while I lay there with my tummy covered in gel. The very patient sonographer at the clinic finally got fed up and suggested that she should write the sex on a piece of paper and pop it into an envelope and so that way, we could open it at our leisure if we felt we wanted to later down the line. Perfect. The scan revealed that the baby was healthy and everything was progressing as normal, so we paid our money and went off to a nearby deli to have a cuppa, obsess over the new scan photos and decide whether to open the envelope or not. We were both back at work before realising that we had left the all-important unopened envelope on the table in the deli! I called, but there was no trace of it. Somebody else out there could know the sex of our baby, but not us. Oh well, it was fate, and deep down, I somehow knew that he was a boy... not because I had a 'feeling' or that it was 'mother's instinct'. It was just because the sonographer had giggled loudly at one point during the scan, and it's fair to say that even at the time of writing this, when Teddy's just six months old, he does have quite a large penis for a baby.

So, there I was in the *One Show* studio and the time had come to tell the viewers my news. My heart quickened and I felt my face flush as Angelica Bell teed up the news. 'Tonight we're asking for your good news stories,' (we love a call out on *The One Show*) 'but I think that we should start with yours, Al.' I could feel my guests, Renée Zellwegger and Sally Phillips, who had come in to talk about their new film, *Bridget Jones's Baby*, looking at me expectantly. Here goes... 'Well...' I started gingerly. 'You couldn't have timed your film more perfectly because my husband and I are thrilled to say that we're expecting a baby.' Just like that, the news was finally out.

The very next day after the announcement, I looked pregnant, as if psychologically I was able to relax and breathe out. I caught myself in my dressing-room mirror as I got changed for the show that evening and there it was, a small, but a very definite bump. I loved it.

A MOVING EXPERIENCE

'That first flutter – words can't even describe it!' Noel

At 22 weeks, I felt little Ted move inside me for the very first time. I wouldn't call it a 'kick', because that's not how it feels at the beginning. I was sitting in the make-up chair at work, and during a rare lull in conversation, I felt a gentle muscle spasm or twitch. Just enough to pique my interest. Then nothing. A few minutes later it happened again, like a goldfish flipping over in my tummy and swimming away. It felt brand new, but familiar at the same time, and I just knew what it was. It's a tough one to describe; most women use the word flutter or liken it to a gas bubble moving. It's so delicate and fleeting at the beginning that it's easy to miss the first few, but as they get more regular you will start to recognise the feeling. Locking yourself in the bathroom and sitting quietly in the bath is a good way to get to know the sensations. **A mother can feel the baby's movement anytime between 18 and 22 weeks, but bear in mind that there are always exceptions.** It was after those first few movements that I noticed my hand constantly hovering over my bump in that way that pregnant women do.

> 'At our first scan I found out that I had an anterior placenta, and that it would be more difficult for me to feel movement – wonderful, something else to worry about!' Mary Jane

The movement becomes stronger and stronger as the weeks pass, until the baby is full on jabbing you in the ribs and back. It's like sitting next to a small person on a bus who is constantly elbowing you in your side or having a very tiny karate black belt practising in your tummy. My favourite pastime in the evening would be placing the remote control on my tummy and watching as Teddy kicked it off.

On occasion, you can even see the movement under your clothes, and while I got used to it, Michael Bublé, who I happened to be interviewing on *The One Show* one evening, spotted my tummy moving and floundered. He lost his thread and got in a right tizz, too embarrassed to explain what had thrown him. Teddy was always quiet in the afternoon, but he would wake up at 7pm on the dot just as the *One Show* titles started playing. It was like an alarm, and towards the end, he was moving so much that I was concerned that some viewers might be a bit freaked out by seeing the shape of a little hand or foot through the fabric of my dress!

Gradually, you will get to know the movement patterns of your baby. **There are some very vague guidelines that suggest that you should feel ten movements every two hours from week 28 but it's definitely not an exact science.**

My instinct told me at week 27 something wasn't quite right. My little wriggler had stopped wriggling, and despite lying quietly, concentrating intently to see whether I could feel something, nothing happened. I downed some lemonade, as suggested on Mumsnet, hoping that the sugar would kick-start some movement, but nothing. With tears stinging my eyes I rang Lisa, my midwife, who advised that I should get checked out at the hospital.

I was sobbing by the time I got there, certain that there was a problem. It was the first time that I really knew what it felt like to worry like a mother and it was unthinkable that something could be wrong. I lay on the bed, monitors strapped to me, waiting, willing any sign of life. After a long and anxious 40 minutes, the familiar kicks started again and I could hear his little heartbeat racing a million beats a minute. I beamed at the midwife, relief flooding through me. Everything was absolutely fine, Ted was just having a longer nap than usual, but I was glad that we had checked. **You have a mother's instinct; never doubt it, always listen to it.**

There are many upsides to being pregnant, apart from the obvious. With the addition of a bump, people are kinder and more generous towards you. They will also use adjectives that I used to find trite and patronising like 'blossoming' and 'glowing', but the good news is that they are telling the truth. You do both blossom and glow at some points. For most of us, hair does become thicker and glossier, skin is clearer and nails are stronger. I don't think it's all pregnancy hormones though; some of it must be down to the fact that alcohol is, for the most part, off the menu.

Alcohol and your pregnancy

Let's talk about alcohol for a minute. The NHS guidelines clearly stipulate that a pregnant woman should avoid alcohol altogether and, of course, we all know that this is the sensible thing to do. However, there is no proof that occasional drinking is hazardous to unborn babies. As much as I enjoy a G&T or a glass of wine of an evening, I chose the safe option and hardly drank at all, but I found it tough to completely abstain for the entire pregnancy. Instead, I would choose my moments carefully: a really good glass of wine with a posh meal or a glass of champagne to toast with on special occasions. I just drank enough to feel that I could join in. Some people are stronger-willed and I respect them for it, but for the rest of us, let's not beat ourselves up about it.

Stop touching me!

One of the most bizarre things about being pregnant is that some people can't seem to stop touching your bump. What is that about? Just think about it for a moment. Would you normally go up to one of your friends, let alone a complete stranger, and stroke her stomach? You just wouldn't, would you? Some guests, male and female, would arrive in the studio before the show, and instead of shaking my hand upon introduction, they'd start patting my belly tenderly, forgetting that I was actually attached. I had all sorts having a go: actors, comedians, a well-known politician, three sirs and even a dame! It was all well meant, I'm sure, just a bit weird.

TIPS AND MORE TIPS

Being pregnant seems to also be an open invitation for others to bombard you with tips. Every guest that sat on the *One Show* sofa had some words of wisdom to offer. Jamie Oliver suggested bringing take-away menus to the hospital so that we could order in some nice food, Mel Giedroyc told me to bathe my nether regions in mineral salts after I gave birth – she even brought me some bless her; even Tom Hanks – yes, *the* Tom Hanks – suggested some books on hypnobirthing, while John Bishop's advice was to enjoy every moment, but to stop at one.

Perineum massage

The most surprising advice, however, came from a friend and colleague who suggested that I may want to start massaging my perineum. Sorry? My what?

Your perineum is the bit of skin between your anus and your vulva. The aim of the game is to massage it with oil at regular intervals from approximately week 34 onwards in order to soften it so that it can stretch more effectively without ripping during labour. The next blow is that it's too difficult to reach it yourself, so you need to ask your partner to do it for you. Enough. Enough. This was a level of intimacy that I wasn't ready for and frankly I'd rather run the risk of a rip.

Stretch marks

One of the best tips I had was from a Glaswegian woman who was a contributor on a programme I was working on. Her words of wisdom were stretchmark-related. Now, while on a good day we try to view stretch marks as a badge of honour, let's be honest, nobody really wants them. She told me that I must moisturise specifically with Clarins oil, the 'Huile Tonic' variety, once a day. I wouldn't normally have paid so much attention, but she was stretchmark-free, having given birth to three – yes, three – sets of twins. To be clear, that's a grand total of six children. They say that genetics play a part in whether or not you get stretch marks, but it was worth a go. I promptly went to purchase the suggested miracle oil and started applying it regularly. It became an obsession. I will warn you that it isn't cheap at £40 a pop, and I went through about four bottles of the stuff. I assume that most body oils would do the job. It's more about the commitment to the cause rather than the product. Another warning: try to avoid running your hands through your hair after rubbing your belly with the oil. I fell foul of this on many occasions and ended up on the telly with a very greasy fringe! However, I am glad to report that it was a sound investment cash- and time-wise because, touch wood, I walked away mostly unscathed.

I just want to sleep

Harder to fix are sleep-related problems. The one thing that you desperately need above anything else when you're pregnant, is a good night's sleep, yet, in a cruel twist of fate, it can be the hardest thing to accomplish. There are many roots to the problem: your bump's too big and you can't get comfortable, sore hips and joints, heartburn, your baby is most active at bedtime and is having an all-night rave in your tummy, you need to pee multiple times a night and can't get back to sleep, or you have a severe cramp in your calf that leads to you leaping out of bed and hopping like a mad person across the bedroom floor.

Apart from having to correct an old habit of sleeping on my back, which is deemed unsafe for the baby after the halfway mark, and the odd cramp that left me wanting to saw my leg off at knee level, I slept relatively well, my daily 4am bathroom visit being the only disturbance.

KEEP YOUR HEARTRATE UP

I put my sleeping well down to the fact that I did some form of exercise most days. I'm not talking 10k runs or a high-intensity session – I'm definitely not one of those superwomen who exercised manically right up until the birth – I just did something to get my heart rate up. Keeping active really helped me enjoy my pregnancy and avoid lots of the painful side effects. I revised my routines on a weekly basis: I stopped running at 18 weeks, replaced that with some gym-based cardio on the cross-trainer and bike, along with some weights, and only did about 25–30 minutes a day. For the last eight weeks, I replaced the gym with brisk walking, which became my go-to activity.

The irony is that while I managed all this when I was pregnant, I've barely put a foot in a trainer since, but those excuses are for another chapter.

I look back on my pregnancy with immense fondness. I felt more at ease with myself than I had in my whole life, I loved not having the pressure to be slim and my bump became a symbol of my new-found purpose. There were some dark days, naturally, but being pregnant brought me a type of happiness and contentment that I'd never experienced before. The best way I can describe it was like the 'Ready Brek' effect. Ted gave me a warm glow right from the start.

Your changing body

It is extraordinary how your body takes on a life of its own during the ten months of pregnancy. It's no surprise, and completely understandable, that lots of women, even those who have been desperate for a child, struggle with being a bystander to their own body, watching it change shape and sometimes texture, without being able to do a single thing about it.

There are plenty of un-pretty parts: the pregnancy shuffle that most of us end up developing in the latter stages, the darkening of moles, which is completely normal, the unwanted appearance of skin folds, and let's not forget that once-neat belly button that gapes and protrudes grotesquely in the last few weeks – panic not, though, it will go back eventually.

Your bump grows and grows, the skin gets tighter and tighter, pushing your organs upwards until your lungs are right under your chin, making it difficult to catch your breath, and tying your own laces becomes an impossible task. It's frustrating and often frightening as you witness your body morphing into a shape that is anything but user-friendly. Sometimes you will find the frustration too much, and that, combined with the pregnancy hormones, can result in anger, tears and some explosive rows between you and your partner, mostly because it's impossible for them to understand how you're feeling. We've all been there. All you can do is accept that the next day will be better.

Being pregnant is like being the subject of your own personal science documentary. It's endlessly fascinating and feeling those kicks is about as special as it gets, and helps you and your baby get to know each other before meeting face to face.

Women may have been having babies for millennia, yet after all these years, nobody is still able to really articulate accurately what it feels like to grow your own son or daughter. It's for you to have your own unique experience.

It's a beautiful, yet fleeting period of time, and despite it being sometimes marred by extreme tiredness, sickness, backache and a whole list of other unpleasantnesses, try your best not to wish it away. Take lots of pictures, keep a diary and embrace it, knowing that you are one of the lucky ones.

FIVE THINGS TO REMEMBER TO HELP YOU THROUGH THE LAST TRIMESTER
Clemmie Hooper, midwife and author
@mother_of_daughters

The last stretch in any pregnancy can feel like an eternity for most women. You can feel like your body is 'all baby', your pelvis aches, your back ache, heck even your fanny aches so here are some things to remember:

Your body is changing shape to allow for this baby to grow. Weight gain is normal; that extra area of padding (especially around your hips and upper arms) is fat stores being laid down for breastfeeding. Try not to get too het up about it all and trust the process.

Sleep is a tricky one as your baby will enjoy using your bladder as a trampoline during the night, which makes regular trips to the loo a common occurrence. Invest in (or borrow) a pregnancy pillow; the best ones are sausage-shaped and can also be used for breastfeeding in the early weeks. My friend loved hers so much she took it on holiday with her and sacrificed essential hand luggage so she could take it on the plane!

Hormones can play havoc with your mind; worrying if you have enough blankets or babygros at 3am is very very normal. Offloading these worries to a close friend or your partner can really help you to make sense of it all. Talking to a fellow mum can make you feel normal – all pregnant women will have gone through this at some point.

4

When writing your birth plan think about it like a birth preference. Birth is unpredictable, and everyone's birth is different. So try not to be set on one idea for pain relief. In the throes of labour anything can change and that includes you.

Pack your hospital bag, then lay it all out on the bed and get your partner to re-pack it. That way he or she knows exactly where everything is, especially in labour when you need that lip balm 'NOW!' Also makes them feel a bit in control of something.

'I am quite an anxious person and worry about everything which gets on all my family's nerves but I absolutely loved being pregnant, my sister even complimented me (which never happens) on how brilliantly I was coping with it and not worrying – she didn't like going out in crowds when she was pregnant. I had waited such a long time for it to happen I just tried to enjoy every second. I had no sickness as long as I kept eating I was fine. I loved my bump and embraced the fact that I could just let my belly hang out and not suck it in. I did have trouble sleeping as every time I moved my back would do a big cracking noise but watching my belly move and kick my husband in the back made it OK! It makes me sad that unfortunately I've been unable to experience it again because pregnancy is so amazing.' Lisa

'Firstly, apart from feeling my baby moving inside me, I didn't enjoy pregnancy one bit. Suffered with extreme tiredness, constantly needing the loo, B12 deficiency & the worst heartburn I've ever experienced! I lived on Rennie's, Gaviscon and Tums!' Lauren

'I had a blissful pregnancy, I was glowing, loving my new body shape, was happy and just so excited to meet my baby!' Caroline

MATERNITY
LEAVE PARANOIA

Finding out that you're pregnant often sparks a very diverse range of emotions and reactions, regardless of your age or how difficult the journey was to get there. The overriding and initial feeling in most cases is joy and elation, but as the dust settles, happiness and hopefulness is sometimes marred by anxiety and apprehension as we realise that a monumental change is afoot.

We all go through phases of worrying about how a new baby might affect our relationships, our social set-up, our finances, but there is often one main culprit at the root of the the worry and that is work. This is especially true of women in their thirties and forties, who are really hitting their career stride and, in many cases, are at the peak of their chosen profession. It's sometimes hard to step back, especially when we know that more than half of all mothers say that pregnancy and maternity leave had a negative effect on their career.

The day that I found out that I was pregnant, I spent the morning on cloud nine, running through lists of possible names, thinking of colour schemes for the nursery and generally getting ahead of myself. That was until I got to work, sat in our usual daily production meeting and gradually, euphoria gave way to anguish as I silently contemplated how a baby was going to impact on my job.

I'm fortunate to work in an environment that's hugely supportive of working parents, an attitude that very much filters down from the man at the top, my boss, Sandy Smith. He has a reputation as a no-nonsense, straight-talking, hard-nosed editor, famed for being in charge of the current affairs giant *Panorama* back in the day, and sometimes he very much is that man, but quietly, he's also a big softie whom his staff adore, me included. I knew that he'd be delighted to hear our news, yet I dreaded telling him and put it off for as long as I could.

At the four-month mark, I knew I had to bite the bullet. My heart was racing as I asked him, as casually as I could muster, whether I could have a quiet word. It was pathetic; I was a 39-year-old woman and yet I felt like a 12-year-old girl who was on her way to see the headmaster. It wasn't Sandy's reaction that I was nervous about; it was the fact that I knew that my news would signal change and talk of maternity leave, something I wanted to ignore for as long as possible.

He followed me out of our open-plan office and into a private meeting room and as I turned to face him, I knew that he had already guessed.

I started: 'So...'

Him, a little smile playing at the corners of his mouth: 'Yes?'

Me: 'Well... the thing is...(I blurted it out)... I'm pregnant and the baby is due in January!'

Him, hugging me: 'That's wonderful news, Al, really great.'

Me, not missing a beat: 'So I'll finish at Christmas, have the baby in January and be back by April?'

A father of four himself, he looked at me questioningly and responded sensibly with 'Let's just see how you feel, shall we?' I appreciated his duty of care, but I had already made my decision. I would take three months of maternity leave and be back on the *One Show* sofa by April, come hell or high water.

I may have been determined, but, in hindsight, I was completely deluded!

I hadn't really stopped to consider how hard it would be to deal with a young baby and juggle work, or even how long it would take me to fully recover and feel well enough to go back. The problem is that you just don't know any of that stuff before you're in it. You think that you have an inkling of how it might be, but actually, you have no bloody idea. What I should have done is asked friends and colleagues who had been there and done it for advice, but instead I panicked, assumed I'd manage somehow and promised too much. I hasten to add though that neither my boss nor the BBC piled any pressure on me; it was all coming from me.

While I was ecstatic to be pregnant, I was petrified of temporarily having to give up a job that I loved. I will freely admit that it pained me to think about someone else in my seat on the show. During my more insecure moments, I agonised over the fact that that my replacements might be better than me and I hated myself for sometimes forgetting to focus on the bigger picture and let this horrible jealousy eat me up.

Luckily, my pregnancy was plain sailing and I felt well, so well that I didn't even consider that I needed to slow down at all, not even as I neared the end of my third trimester. I was still whizzing about at a million miles per hour, living as chaotic a life as I had a year previously. My mother begged me to slow down, to give myself time to rest, but her advice fell on deaf ears, and on I went like a rotund Duracell bunny not wanting to stop 'till I popped'. While I enjoy my job, and the chaos that comes with it, I knew deep down that my raison d'être was the fact that subconsciously I wanted to make a mark while I was still visible.

Some people still don't want to hear women talk about career anxiety when they fall pregnant. It's as if the consensus is: 'for goodness' sake, you've fallen pregnant, what more do you want? Just get on with it and deal with the consequences'. The stigma is very much still there. Oh to be a man.

The point is that most women experience feelings of insecurity about their maternity leave (unless they absolutely detest their job) and those feelings are very much justified. By the age of thirty-something, we've worked long and hard to get to a certain point in our career, and although a baby and family is often way more important, and actually for some the ultimate goal, it's also OK to want to protect a career that you've worked hard to carve out for yourself.

Most big businesses and corporations these days certainly talk a good game when it comes to showing support for men and women but few companies are like Netflix, who have recently announced that they will support any male or female employee on full salary for up to 12 months of leave. The atmosphere in some workplaces still seems somewhat stuck in the 1970s and derogatory towards new mothers. Women who put their families first are still being sidelined for promotions and eyebrows are still being raised when parents are having to leave on time to pick up their children from nursery, etc. Things are getting better, but it's a slow burner and these attitudes are confidence-crushing and can be career-ending.

> 'I went back to full-time work when Emily and Yonatan were six months old, as I always thought that I would want to keep progressing my career even when I became a mum. I quickly realised that in the new situation work needed to have a much bigger impact, meaning and purpose to be worth the effort and the price I had to pay for not being with my family. I found that in Zinc – my new venture, which combines entrepreneurship, tech and social impact. For those who want family and career – try to think about "integrating" rather than "balancing" the two. The other secret is to choose a really great partner who will support you and your choices!' Ella Goldner, Co-founder of Zinc

There is no doubt about it; maternity leave not only means temporarily leaving your job, but it also signals the beginning of significant financial change. Regardless of your circumstances, you will need to think about budgeting while you're off work because from here on in, two wages gradually become one, with statutory maternity pay hopefully helping you cover the basics. The average length of maternity leave in the UK is 39 weeks and it's at every company's discretion to decide how much they will contribute to their employee's leave. Some have a full nine months' paid maternity, but it's not the norm.

Adjusting to managing on less income can be tough and can take some getting used to, especially if you're used to being financially independent. It can impact relationships and put extra strain on this already unpredictable situation. Three friends of mine who are freelancers and the highest earners in their family took jobs on at two, three and eight weeks respectively after giving birth. They weren't completely 'back at work', so to speak, but they took one-off jobs that were lucrative and that would help fund their unpaid maternity leave. People whispered behind their backs about it being too soon, they made judgements about them without understanding their circumstances or walking a day in their shoes. I found it incredibly disrespectful, especially as it was a necessity and not a choice. But even if it were a choice, what is with the judging? Each person is entitled to make a decision based on what feels right for them.

'As a headteacher, the decision not to go back to work wasn't really an option financially nor really was a part-time return but to be honest, that was difficult too as I really enjoyed my work. The weight on my shoulders of leaving my first son with someone else to head to work was always heavy, but was offset time and time again by walking in at the end of the day: the smile and recognition of my baby when he saw me made my heart burst every time and was almost worth that heavy feeling. Now, just a few years later, I appreciate that they need to go to school so the feeling of leaving them isn't so bad. What I would say is that it's about decisions and choices. My decision would not be the best decision for another new mum but try not to compare yourselves to others; the important people in your life know you and respect your reasons. I asked them if they minded if I worked and within a heartbeat, they answered no Mummy, you're teaching us that you need to work for things in life and we want to be good at our jobs like you are at yours.' Ruth

My last appearance on *The One Show* before my maternity leave was an emotional affair. I was 38 weeks pregnant and Gary Barlow and Mel Giedroyc waved me off as I said a tearful goodbye, or should I say au revoir? My ankles and feet swollen, I waddled from the studio into a waiting cab, armed with a massive card from all the staff at the show and an impressive bouquet of flowers. It was time to for me to nest, and physically I was exhausted, yet psychologically, I was still struggling to let go.

My last day!

Earlier that day, the *Watchdog* team were sharing our make-up room and I arrived to find their presenter, Sophie Raworth, in the chair. Straight to the point, she asked me how much maternity time I was planning on taking. 'Three months or so,' I answered, unsure of what the right answer should be. She politely stopped the make-up artist in her tracks and swivelled the chair around so that she could look me straight in the eye. 'Really?' I was confused. Was that a good or bad thing? 'That is no time at all, Alex, and it will disappear in a flash,' she said, which answered my question. She told me how she had felt the same pressure to return quickly when she was pregnant but regretted rushing back shortly after her first child was born.

I obviously still looked unconvinced, because she said one of the kindest things that any colleague has ever said, which was 'Just remember, Alex, that nobody out there can do your job like you can. That sofa will be waiting for you whenever you're ready.' I lunged forward and hugged her for an uncomfortable amount of time, her newly applied foundation smearing my tent-like dress. It wasn't necessarily true, but a lovely sentiment that raised my spirits regardless. She quickly added, 'but under no circumstances should you try to watch the programme while you're on maternity leave. It will serve no other purpose than torturing you for no good reason.'

I heeded her advice and from the very first day of maternity leave I made a conscious effort to avoid BBC One at 7pm. It had an immediate effect, and from that first afternoon of leave, any thoughts about work melted away, and the new baby became my sole focus. So my tip to you would be to turn off all work email notifications the minute you leave.

I had planned to have a clear two weeks off before Teddy was due to make an appearance. I thought that would be an ample amount of time and, as everybody kept saying, 'the first baby is always late.' Well as it turns out, that is complete bullshit. The first baby is in fact not always late and Teddy appeared just a week later at 39 weeks. The problem was that I had spent the first week running around like a headless chicken, banking on having at least another week, if not more, to relax and put my feet up. That didn't happen. Instead, labour happened and then I was in charge of a brand-new baby who didn't seem to have got the memo that his new mama was already knackered!

Please do not make the same mistake. **Overestimate how much time you need to prepare physically and mentally before your new baby is born because that is literally the last chance you will ever have to put yourself first.** Taking an extra week before your due date won't have any impact on your work life, but it will make the world of difference to how prepared you feel when those first contractions hit. Be selfish; this is your time.

> 'I couldn't believe how many people in the office asked me when I would be back after giving birth; I really felt the pressure. I'm due to go on maternity leave soon, and have found the last few weeks really stressful – there's just so much to do, I'm worried about being exhausted before I've even begun! To add to the stress,

we still haven't found a maternity cover for my role, which makes the expectation to come back early even higher. My husband and I are both at a senior level, and it does feel like we're being pulled in a million different directions.' Sarah

HELEN, THE GUILTY MOTHERS CLUB, @GUILTYMOTHER BLOG

Pregnancy & maternity discrimination takes many forms and impacts a startling number of women. Know firstly that this is not your fault, you are not alone and there is help available. Organisations like Pregnant then Screwed provide a free legal helpline so if you are in any doubt about whether the way you are being treated is fair then give them a ring and ask the question.

ESSENTIALS – THE LIST OF ALL THE LISTS

Our house, apart from the kitchen, is a bit bare, as we don't really have much furniture. Some rooms are completely empty. Our hamsters (our eldest children) have the dining room all to themselves, apart from an old rickety piano that we acquired from my boss's mother. You see, we moved into our house after a mammoth renovation just three weeks before Teddy was born and, as some of you know and the rest will soon find out, home decor is pushed way, way down the list of priorities once you have a baby-in-arms.

We had no furniture, but at least we had plenty of space and slowly but surely, square inch by square inch, our house has been filled with baby equipment. While Charlie and I are making do with a couple of mismatched chairs, Teddy wants for nothing. His every need, want and whim is catered for and I'm now very glad that we have the space for the mammoth amount of paraphernalia that accompanies a baby.

Eight months into the pregnancy though, we had nothing, not a car seat, a babygro, or even a nappy. It wasn't because we were superstitious; we just struggled to find the time amid working full-time, trying to deal with builders, which is like herding cats, and moving back into the house.

There really wasn't any need to panic though – we spent one whole night researching products online (**MadeForMums is a very comprehensive and easy-to-use website**) and then a trip to the baby department at John Lewis the following day and it was done; we had the basics.

You may not want to make it quite so last-minute and you may prefer to spread the cost to help your cash flow, especially as your maternity leave is looming. For many bits and pieces we relied on friends and relatives for hand-me-downs. I admit that it is nice to buy some brand-new stuff for your little human, and some things like car seats and cot mattresses can't be second-hand for safety reasons, but just remember that babies move through each stage at the speed of light and many friends and siblings, especially if they've had more than one child, will be very keen to re-home some equipment, so think about who you could source some things from before you buy everything from new and spend a fortune. **Make a budget and stick to it.**

As well as what we bought, we were lucky enough to be given lots of products to try that we were extremely grateful for, so by thinking about what we used and didn't, and by comparing notes with tons of other parents, I have collated some lists that will hopefully help lighten the load and be a starting point for you.

NOTEBOOKS AT THE READY... PREPARATION

First things first. Prepping. You'll need to make some space.

The best piece of advice I had pre-baby was to declutter

before I bought a single thing. Luckily, we had no clutter – it was all in storage – but I absolutely agree that this is a very good place to start. Be ruthless because you'll need space for baby-related objects in pretty much every room, apart from guest rooms, so think about some drawers, cupboards, shelves or surface space that you're able to free up in anticipation. By the way, I am the last person who should be dishing out advice like this as Charlie and I were extremely disorganised, but with the help of Mary the Mighty (my mum) and through absolute necessity, we learnt pretty damn quickly that we would need to put some systems in place and get ourselves organised if we were going to survive the first six months.

So have a good look at your home. Ask yourself where you'll keep most of the baby's kit. Some would automatically assume that the best place would be the nursery, but equipment like a bouncer or a 'jumparoo' is much more useful in, say, the kitchen where you can get on with some chores while the baby is entertained in a safe place.

You'll need to pay particular attention to areas like the hallway. What size pram can you get through? Measure the width of the front and back doors to see what will fit. Simple, I know, but many couples we know – including us – completely forgot and had to swap to a different make of buggy or pram at the last minute. Think about where you might store your buggy, especially on rainy days when you just want to get into the house without collapsing the whole thing.

Look at your bedroom and imagine a crib next to the bed. Yes, it's definitely time to get rid of that huge pile of magazines that's currently there. Also, if you live in a house, consider having two well-stocked changing areas, one upstairs and one downstairs, if only for the first few weeks, as the last thing you'll want to do is tackle the stairs more often than necessary when you're tired and sore.

NOW TO THE BUYING...

This is undoubtedly the most exciting part of the preparation and it's very easy to get carried away when you suddenly find yourself in the baby department surrounded by teeny-tiny velour babygros. You will also be dazzled by the endless possibilities of products from cribs to car seats, strollers to sterilisers and, like us, you will assume that you need more than you actually do. All the sensible spending habits that you have learnt and lived by over the years will vanish and the urge to overprovide for your new being will come on strong. Your first task is to recognise these feelings when they surface and put the brakes on – before handing over your credit card. Do not spend like a lottery winner in Harrods, there's no need.

Many people will decide to really go for it and create a beautiful nursery for the new arrival well in advance. With endless choices of nursery furniture and fabrics on the market I know how tempting that is. Just remember that you really won't need a nursery for the first few months as your baby will be sleeping in your room, and although it could serve as a handy changing area, if you're anything like us you'll find that you'll mainly use your own bedroom for feeding, changing and sleeping.

We hardly set foot in our nursery until Teddy was six months old and ready to sleep in his own cot. We had painted the room in advance and had set up his cot and changing area, but everything else in terms of furniture and decoration has been added bit by bit. **So don't panic if your nursery isn't ready for the new arrival and just consider that creating the perfect nursery in advance, while an exciting project, could be a substantial cost that you could easily spread over the first year.**

So what about the things that you do need? Well let's start at the very beginning.

YOUR HOSPITAL CHECKLIST

I'm sure lots of friends will send you their version of the 'hospital bag list'. You can edit them all together or pick one from a trusted source and stick to it. I used a list that was sent to me by my agent Laura, because she is the most organised and no-nonsense person who has ever graced this earth. Fact. She even sent a short-stay and a long-stay version. Did I mention anal? Anyway, I've edited it a bit and added some modifications. Warning. Lots of items on the list are less than attractive! Us women are so lucky...

Baby clothes

In the absence of a crystal ball you will need to buy two sizes for your new baby: 'tiny baby' and 'newborn'. I didn't even realise that 'tiny baby' was an actual size, but it turns out that that is what most babies wear during their first fortnight on planet Earth. For example, Ted was born at 7lbs 11oz and fitted perfectly into the tiny baby size for at least the first two to three weeks, especially as he, like many babies, lost ten per cent of his birth weight after birth. Some people think that you should wash all baby clothes before they're worn, but try to keep some in the packaging just in case the size doesn't fit and you need to take them back.

- 2 x packs of long- or short-sleeve COTTON VESTS, depending on the time of year that your new arrival is due.
- 2 x packs of plain white SLEEPSUITS/BABYGROS. I opted for towelling ones as they feel so nice and wash particularly well. (I'm starting to sound like my mum.)
- I also bought 2 x 'GOING HOME' BABYGROS that were a bit more special.
- 2 x woollen CARDIGANS in case it's cold.
- 2 x BABY HATS. All their heat escapes through their heads so it's important to make sure that they have a hat on, especially in winter.
- 2 x packs of BABY MITTS. (Optional; you may prefer to turn over the in-built mitts that are often on the sleepsuits.)
- 1 x SNOWSUIT if you're taking the baby home in cold weather.

It is pointless to spend lots of money on pretty and intricate babygros for the early days as you will need to change your baby upwards of three times a day, so practical stuff that can handle a hot washing-machine cycle is what you need.

Baby essentials

◇ MUSLIN CLOTHS

Buy stacks and stacks of muslin cloths and pack as many as possible into your hospital bag. You can never have enough.

> 'Muslin squares – just soooo many muslin squares, I use them for everything!' Jamie

◇ A PACK OF COTTON WOOL BALLS

◇ A SMALL BOTTLE OF OLIVE OIL

Just decant some from your cupboard. This will help remove the first tar-like poo called meconium that your baby will pass in the first few days.

◇ NAPPIES FOR TINY BABY AND NEWBORN

◇ A CELLULAR BLANKET

◇ SMALL BOTTLES OR CARTONS OF FORMULA

You'll need bottles if you're planning on bottle-feeding or just in case you find breastfeeding impossible, and a couple of microwave steam sterilising kits will save carrying an actual steriliser.

◇ CAR SEAT

You will not be allowed to leave the hospital without one, whether you're travelling home in your own car or by taxi. After picking up every single car seat in the shop to test how heavy/ sturdy they were, we opted for the lightest that a very reputable brand had to offer and thank goodness we did! The already heavy seat will only get heavier once there's a growing baby in it. Hauling Ted to the surgery at nine months in his car seat was like moving a dead weight, and most babies are in their first seat for the first 15 months, so don't just think about getting your newborn home, really think about the practicalities of getting a one-year-old in and out of the car. Most big brands now offer an iso-fix system, which means that you can slot the seat in and out of the car without having to fiddle about with seat belts, and I can tell you that when it's hammering down with rain and you're trying to get your child into the car, the extra bit of cash spent is well worth it.

Essentials for you

◇ PYJAMAS...

... at least two sets. Pick some that are button-down so that you have easy access for feeding and a pair that you are happy to be photographed in! N.B. It's quite tricky to tick both these boxes with the one set so some good research will be required.

◇ DRESSING GOWN

A nice cotton one would be ideal. Nothing too heavy for those warm wards at the hospital.

◇ NIGHTIE

Again, choices are limited, but pick a T-shirt style in a dark colour as you'll need something to put on shortly after giving birth. Without being too graphic, it's a messy couple of hours after the birth. You may never want to wear it again, but see it as a pit stop between nakedness and your photograph-worthy PJs.

◇ BLACK PANTS

2 x packs. You will wear these in the hospital and for the first few weeks post-partum. The other option is incredibly sexy J-cloth pants. They're one size fits all, so will be perfect after birth and will shrink with your tummy. They're inexpensive, can be bought from Amazon and, importantly, you wear them once and throw them away. I preferred proper cotton knickers if I'm honest.

> 'I couldn't live without my disposable knickers – I bled a little after the birth and these were a life saver, much comfier than a pad.' Ella

◇ MATERNITY SANITARY TOWELS

I would recommend Optimama Pura. Some of the other brands leave you feeling a bit sticky and sweaty, which is a bridge too far in this already gruesome aftermath.

◇ 2 X MATERNITY BRAS

◇ FLIP-FLOPS

Don't be tempted to take slippers as maternity wards are hot as hell, and you will also want to wear your flip-flops to the shower. Slippers will get wrecked for reasons we won't get into.

◇ AN OUTFIT TO LEAVE THE HOSPITAL

Think about soft fabrics, not jeans with buttons, as everything will feel a bit tender. Take a top that will button up in case you end up having a C-section; the gas they give you can sometimes cause pain in your shoulders so this sort of top is kinder.

◇ SHOES THAT ARE EASY TO SLIP ON (some boots during winter or pumps in the summer)

◇ A BRUSH AND SOME HAIR TIES

◇ SHAMPOO, CONDITIONER AND SHOWER GEL

Choose products that you love for that first shower post-birth. A familiar smell can be immensely comforting.

◇ FACE WIPES

◇ A REALLY GOOD MOISTURISER AND LIP BALM

A hot hospital ward + gas and air + blood loss = very dry everything!

◇ TOOTHPASTE AND TOOTHBRUSH

◇ YOUR MAKE-UP BAG

The pictures taken just after you've given birth will haunt you for the rest of your life and while you will not feel like applying anything more than some blusher and a quick coat of mascara, you will be glad that you did when your child is 18 and that first picture is blown up and stuck on the wall of the pub where your son or daughter is having their birthday bash.

◇ CAMERA AND CHARGER

◇ PHONE AND CHARGER

◇ SNACKS AND DRINKS

Choose easily digestible bite-sized food, like pieces of pineapple or watermelon, that will be cooling during labour and some healthy bars or jelly sweets that will boost your energy. Post-birth you will be ready for some comfort food. Think about treats. Chocolate bars to go with a cuppa are always welcome Drinks-wise, coconut water is excellent for rehydrating and means that you won't need to go to the toilet as often. Take straws to make drinking during labour a bit easier.

◇ YOUR MATERNITY NOTES

Anything else that's not on that list is not essential.

So, picture the scene: you've just returned home from the hospital and you're both staring cluelessly at your new son or daughter, who is still ensconced in the car seat. Your adventure is just beginning, and these are the absolute must-haves for your first 12 weeks:

WHAT YOU NEED AT HOME

SLEEPING

▷ A CRIB OR MOSES BASKET

We used a 'snuzpod', which we loved. It fitted neatly into the bedroom and because it attached to my side of the bed it made reaching for Ted in the night to feed him, or just to comfort him, a lot easier. The downside is that it's also very heavy, so although you can use it as a bassinet for daytime naps, it's difficult to move, especially for mums who have had a C-section. Therefore, we also had a very lightweight Moba Moses basket for downstairs, which was a luxury and a life saver, as we could move it to the kitchen or lounge depending on where we were. N.B. Your baby will only sleep in the Moba up to four months and less in a Moses basket, depending on his or her size. As soon as Ted outgrew his, we started putting him down for naps in his cot so that he would get used to it before we finally moved him into his own nursery.

▷ 2 X FITTED SHEETS FOR YOUR CRIB/MOSES BASKET

▷ SWADDLE CLOTHS/LARGE MUSLIN CLOTHS

We swaddled Teddy up until he was three months old and he was a good sleeper.

▷ 3 X SLEEPING BAGS AGE 0–6 MONTHS

Get ones that vary in weight, depending on the time of year that you will be using them. It's worth considering finding one where you can unzip the feet section without having to unzip the whole thing.

⊳ BLANKETS

Either lightweight cotton or heavier cellular ones, depending on the time of year. You will probably receive some of these as gifts too so just buy one for the hospital and then wait and see what you get. You will generally need about four in total as you will use them when you're out and about with the pram or stroller too.

⊳ COMFORTERS

This is a personal choice and not all babies find them helpful, but it's definitely worth a go.

⊳ 5+ DUMMIES

Ever contentious; some parents love them and some loathe them. The fact is it's easier to break a dummy habit than a thumb-sucking habit. We used a dummy at the beginning and slowly weaned Teddy off so that by six months he could fall asleep without one. It definitely helped him sleep in the beginning but we spent A LOT of time putting the dummy back in his mouth in the early days when it would fall out, hence eventually weaning him off. It's for everybody to feel their own way on this one. After much trial and error, we found that the NUK dummies seemed to suit a younger baby better, and the glow-in-the-dark ones are a life saver at 4am!

⊃ A COT

You obviously won't need this at the beginning, but it's a good idea to start putting your baby down for naps in one once you feel he or she is ready so that the transition to their own room will be less traumatic when the time comes.

⊃ COT MATTRESS

This should come with the cot, but if you're like us and opt for a hand-me-down cot, you will need a new mattress. The Little Green Sheep company make great organic mattresses and bedding.

⊃ 2 X FITTED SHEETS FOR THE COT

⊃ A BABY MONITOR

Many would say that a video monitor is their preferred choice as it lets you see the child and therefore restricts the number of times you have to get out of bed in the night. Video monitors also help you to learn about your baby's sleeping habits, therefore giving you a better understanding of their routine. We have an audio monitor that was a hand-me-down from my sister. She used it with both her children with no problems and we find that it's sufficient for us. (We're also too tight to buy a new one, but you never know, we may cave and go video at some point.)

BATHING

⊃ BODY AND HAIR WASH

A gentle, chemical-free body and hair wash (although some people choose not to bathe their baby, just 'topping and tailing' for the first two weeks).

⊃ SPONGES x 2

⊃ COMB AND SOFT BRUSH

⊃ BABY OIL to treat dry skin

⊃ TOWELS x 3

Again, you may receive some of these as gifts, so start with just the one, but don't be tempted to use your own towels. Wash them separately too. The very cute towels with hoods are brilliant for keeping your baby warm.

You can bathe your baby single-handedly, but it can be a two-parent job until you get to grips with it! Failing that, bath seats are easy and cheap to come by. We used a second-hand Mothercare ergonomic bath seat, which new is only £15.00, and it did make bathtime a lot more fun for Teddy as he could enjoy the water for longer. As he got older, we moved onto the Safety 1st swivel bath seat from John Lewis, which again was a hand-me-down from a friend, but it's £13.00 new. Not essential, but nice to have.

CLOTHING

▷ 10—15 TINY BABY OR NEWBORN SLEEPSUITS AND LONG-/ SHORT-SLEEVE VESTS

Opt for plain colours and multipacks as you will be changing your new baby so often. Also remember that you will be inundated with gifts, most of which will be clothing for 0-3 months, so you just need to buy the basics to keep you going until these fit. My tip would be to stick to comfy sleepsuits for the first eight weeks. It's tempting, with so much insanely beautiful baby clothing on the market, to buy mini pairs of jeans, dresses and tiny shirts, but just consider how uncomfortable poppers and zips can be for new babies who spend most of their time on their back. There will be plenty of time for dressing up later.

▷ HATS

A hat is essential in all seasons, whether to stop heat loss through the head or to shade from the sun.

▷ SOCKS

You won't need many pairs in the early days as your baby will mainly be in sleepsuits but from three months on, the need is greater. The trick is to find ones that don't slide off. I'm still looking for the perfect pair!

MILK

⊳ BREAST PUMP

If you're planning on breastfeeding, you'll need a breast pump. It's not exactly the height of sophistication, and makes you feel like you should be standing on all fours in a barn, but it's necessary. Speak to your midwife about when you should start using it. I used the Medela Symphony. Plug it into the mains, though, otherwise you will go through batteries like nobody's business. I tried a hand pump, and frankly found it useless, but each to their own.

I didn't bother buying a feeding chair, so it's not an absolute essential, but I wish I had. My bed and sofa weren't conducive to feeding and I ended up with a very sore back, which, let me tell you, you need like a hole in the head on top of everything else. Many of my friends favoured the Ikea 'Poang' chair, which is a fair price at £95.

⊳ STERILISER

Everyone needs one eventually, but you'll need it immediately if you decide to bottle- or to combination-feed from the kick-off. We use the Avent Steam Steriliser, which has been worth every penny. Ours came with eight bottles, four small ones for the early days and four larger ones, which meant that we haven't had to buy any more. It also came with a bottle brush, which is key. Be sure to have a bottle of white wine vinegar to hand as you will need to clean the steaming tray every other day or so.

▷ FORMULA

Even if you are hell-bent on breastfeeding, do have a couple of bottles of formula to hand or a box of powder. It's just good backup in case you find feeding excruciating and feel better psychologically knowing that you have some to hand should the worst happen. Plus it also means that Dad can be involved, but lots of midwives are very much against combination feeding until your breastfeeding is established so it's really up to you to make your own call on that.

▷ MUSLIN CLOTHS

As many as you can afford and scatter them all over the house so that there is always one to hand.

▷ MATERNITY BRAS

▷ BREAST PADS

▷ BREAST CREAM

Lansinoh cream for sore and cracked nipples. Failing that, you can use Vaseline.

▷ A PLASTIC JUG OR VESSEL

You'll need this to warm expressed or formula milk as microwaving can create hot spots.

NAPPY CHANGING

I'd suggest two well-stocked changing stations, especially if you live in a house on more than one floor, which include:

▷ CHANGING MATS

▷ WIPES

We use water wipes as they're the most natural you can buy, but we used cotton wool and cooled boiled water for changing for the first three months.

▷ NAPPIES

▷ NAPPY RASH CREAM

Sudocrem is good, but I preferred a balm from a small independent company called Jeanvie that cleared up any rash immediately.

▷ NAPPY SACKS

It's non-essential, but we use the Angelcare nappy system, which seals dirty nappies, meaning that it's very hygienic and makes it easy to dispose of them.

▷ MILTON ANTIBACTERIAL WIPES

OUT AND ABOUT
▷ PRAM OR STROLLER

The variety available in terms of brands, style, weight, size and price is brain-melting. This bit of kit is a real investment piece that you may use for years and years and potentially for multiple children, so choose wisely. As I said, measure your doors, do your research and consider the life you lead.

- Do you need to take it on public transport?
- If you have a car, how large is the boot?
- If you live in a flat, do you need to haul it upstairs or is there a lift?
- Is the lift big enough?
- Will you spend time in the countryside where you may need something a bit sturdier?
- Do you intend to jog with the buggy?
- If your chosen buggy comes with a bassinet, will you have room to store it when you're finished with it?

Read reviews to find out which model would be better for your needs, go to a department store to try a variety of models and then pick one carefully. You may be interested to know that some hold their value better than others if you need to sell it down the line. N.B. A sheepskin to pop in the seat is ideal for keeping your baby snuggly in winter and cool in summer but you will get by without if you need to.

'We've got so much use out of our little sheepskin rug – it really helps to soothe Rosa.' Karen

SLING

Essential if you have a baby who hates being put down. It gives you freedom to get on with some chores at home and is great for taking baby out without the drama of a buggy.

CHANGING BAG

You may get one with your pram or stroller. This is essential for going out and about as it will also include a changing mat. Keep it well stocked at all times and invest in a neoprene thermal bag to pop inside so that you can keep milk at a specific temperature or little pots of food when you're weaning later on.

ADAPTORS FOR THE CAR SEAT

These will allow you to attach your car seat to the base of your stroller, which is ideal when you need to pop into the supermarket or to pay for petrol. Check which adaptors will work on your pram as they aren't universal.

TOYS

⇨ MOBILE

A mobile above the cot and changing area is a great distraction, especially when nappy changing gets trickier at around six months.

⇨ FABRIC STRIPS

With black-and-white and coloured pictures that you can put inside the Moses basket or bassinet of the pram will help with entertaining in the early days.

⇨ BABY GYM

It's really worth checking eBay and charity shops for this bit of kit – lots of parents get gifted more than one, so it's relatively easy to pick one up second-hand, still in its packaging!

⇨ SMALL MOBILE

That can hang on the car seat for long journeys.

⇨ TOMY STAR

It is a great help to signal bedtime and to help with sending Teddy off to sleep.

FOR WHEN YOUR BABY GETS BIGGER...

⟩ BOUNCER OR SWING CHAIR

You will quickly realise that it's impossible to carry your new baby around all day and having places to put them down during the day when they're not yet ready to nap is a godsend; be sure you wait until your baby can hold their head up without any assistance for 20 minutes before introducing a bouncer. NHS guidelines advise not leaving them in a bouncer for more than 20 minutes.

By four to five months, your baby will need more stimulation and exercise. We chose the Jumparoo (though not for everyone) and bought a second-hand one for £25 on Gumtree. A good clean with some antibacterial spray and it was as good as new.

⟩ THERMOMETER

⟩ ROOM TEMPERATURE GAUGE

We were given a Gro Egg as a gift and have used it ever since. We rely on it when deciding what to dress Teddy in to go to bed and which sleeping bag to use.

This list took me a long time to compile as I really wanted to get it right for you. I struggled when I was pregnant to find information on what I needed to buy and I didn't find any websites that were consistent so I'm hoping that this will save you a lot of time scouring the internet, allowing more time for the important stuff likc... ahem ... putting your feet up. Now go forth and photocopy!

TO NCT OR NOT NCT

'I don't need or want any new friends.'

That was the opening gambit of a no-nonsense, straight-talking Mexican and one of the other mothers-to-be who Charlie and I met on our NCT course.

She was dead against the sugar-coated ideal that you can make friends for life at NCT. To be fair, many don't and it's not necessarily for everyone, but fast forward nine months and she's well and truly in our gang. She fell hook, line and sinker for us and admits that she may have been hasty.

The thing is that we all have plenty of friends, too many to keep up with at times – school friends, uni friends, work friends – but the truth is that when you have a baby, you will need new ones. You'll still love your old friends and nobody can replace them, but for the first year after having a baby, it's highly likely that you'll see them a lot less. In the meantime, you'll need some new friends who can empathise completely with this new-fangled baby situation that you've found yourself in. Old friends who have children will try to remember the early stages, but will never have as much clarity as parents who are experiencing exactly the same stuff at exactly the same time as you.

Some told us that NCT is a waste of time; others said that we might as well give it a go but it was unlikely we'd find anybody we wanted to be proper friends with. One friend summed it up by saying that it's an expensive way to buy friends, but worth every penny. She hit the nail on the head. It is expensive, and a bit middle class, but it was the best £240 that we ever spent. You can and probably will make other friends elsewhere – in baby classes, for example – but doing an NCT class will give you a solid foundation, and there are discounts available, as Sarah will talk about shortly.

I was always keen on attending NCT classes. As well as needing support because we have no family in London and most of my close friends who have children are also back in Wales, we didn't have the first idea about how to look after a baby.

SARAH BRADLEY,
Antenatal Teacher and NCT Lead

'If I had to recommend NCT based on just one thing, it would be the confidence that it helps new parents to build. Just meeting other people who are in a similar situation is a huge help – remember, you are not alone! Concessions and discounts are available for parents in receipt of benefits or on lower incomes too – it's always worth asking at your local NCT group for more information.

Overall, my top three reasons to go would be:
1. The confidence-building!
2. It really is a brilliant place to meet new friends.

3. It is a very friendly and safe space to learn more about what can sometimes be, let's face it, a pretty daunting prospect.

Everyone is in the same boat, and there are no stupid questions.'

OUR NCT EXPERIENCE

We booked an intense weekend course in the second week of December at 32 weeks pregnant. Lots of people prefer to spread classes over the course of a few weeks to avoid information overload and because they find it easier to make friends over a longer period of time, but due to work commitments that wasn't an option for us. We needed to cram it in and just hoped that everyone else would be up for making friends quickly.

Tensions were running high on the morning of the first day and we were running late. The night before the big day we had all been sent an email with an itinerary and a request to bring snacks. On the way, we stopped in Sainsbury's and stood in the biscuit aisle for an extraordinary amount of time bickering about which variety might impress our future friends the most. We eventually went with some Jaffa Cakes (neither cake nor biscuit), plus some tangerines, just to give the impression that we were a bit health-conscious too, then I waddled as fast as I could, desperate not to be the last couple to arrive, to the centre where our course was being held.

We arrived with a minute to spare, hot, sweaty and flustered, despite it being a bitter winter morning. Everyone was comically polite as we made small talk while standing awkwardly around the rusty urn in the kitchen area. Glancing from behind our steaming polystyrene cups of tea, we tried to get the measure of each other before Sarah, our NCT teacher, called time and invited us all to sit in a circle where we would spend 16 hours over the course of two days, learning how to become parents and – more importantly – looking for new mates who would share the ups and downs of the next few months.

First up was the obligatory introductions. Nervously and self-consciously, each couple introduced themselves and shared with the group when their baby was due and at which hospital they would be giving birth. While each pair stood up the rest of us assessed, made assumptions – a cattle market for parents-to-be.

To our right there was Cara and David, a studious-looking French couple who had come armed with a notebook – obviously organised; next to them, Jess and Paul, a Canadian and American combo who seemed to be no-nonsense and wanted to get the job done; to their right, Lexie and Jack, her English and him Australian – they weren't complete strangers as Charlie and Jack already knew each other – then there was Marissa, who I instantly liked, and her softly spoken British husband Dan; Ise and Carlos, her a Norwegian handball champion and him Italian, who looked capable and cool as cucumbers – just as well with twins on the way; and finally Sai and Reena, a very sweet Indian couple who looked as nervous as we felt. We were like the United Nations.

> 'The other people in our class were quite a bit younger than us, and everything was Pinterest this, Instagram that. I felt a bit like a fish out of water: everything we had was second-hand and I was more concerned about the baby than the nursery colour scheme!' Sarah

What happens at NCT

With introductions done it was time to get down to the nitty gritty. 'So, let's start with the birth,' announced Sarah, a stylish, approachable fifty-something and mother of three, who, armed with flip charts, props and various visual aids, took us seamlessly through the fundamentals of what the next few months had in store for us.

In the first few hours, 14 successful adults, all mid-thirties to early forties, morphed into a classroom of school children, too shy to ask questions and giggling childishly at references to vaginas. It transpired that despite all of us having successful careers, we were very sketchy on what lay ahead. It was an even playing field and instantly our desperate lack of knowledge became the building blocks for the friendships that have developed since.

We started right at the beginning with labour. It was the first time that most of us had heard a proper run-down of what was in store: the contractions, the breathing techniques, the various stages, crowning and eventually the birth. Faces around the room were a picture. Sarah encouraged questions, of which we had hundreds.

Midway through explaining the various stages of labour, Sarah reached the intense transition phase. She explained that this would happen when we reached eight centimetres dilated, and said, 'At that point, you will probably feel like you want to jump out of the window.' That was the ice-breaker because self-confessed hypochondriac and pain-phobic Marissa erupted with a John McEnroe-esque: 'You cannot be serious!' From then on, the floodgates were open and everyone gradually felt at ease enough to air all their concerns, no matter how significant or trivial, and Sarah competently and honestly answered all our queries. Nothing was off-limits, well, apart from perineum massage, which was a bit much for some of the menfolk.

After lunch, it was time to get practising, and each couple were handed their very own 'baby'. Exactly like *The Generation Game*, we all followed Sarah as she showed us how to change a nappy, how to swaddle, how to bathe and the many ways to wind a baby. I wasn't the only thirty-something who had never done any of the above. There was a lot of laughter as we compared each other's clumsy efforts. It was bizarre how we all reacted to having a plastic doll as if the reality of what was ahead was finally sinking in. Having gently swaddled 'Baby Annabel', Charlie cradled her against his chest like she was the most precious thing in the world, and it was only when Sarah nudged him that it was time to put the dolls back in the storage box at the end of the session that he twigged. The NCT weekend definitely helped him to mentally start making that transition from childless man to father. It was during that weekend that it really dawned on Charlie that things were about to change drastically, and the course really helped to fire up his excitement and interest.

'It dawned on me that I'd never held a baby before, so during a visit to a toy store I bought a doll – not for a baby or a child, but for me, what was happening to me. It was a perfect plan, and under the cover of darkness, curtains drawn, I practised changing their nappy, babygro, winding, soothing and anything else I thought I may have to do. I had no idea if it was like the real thing or not, but it boosted my self-esteem no end.'
Ashley

We crammed a lot of information into those two days and, aided by a shared appetite to learn and a lot of humour, we all left feeling much better equipped to deal with what was ahead. The camaraderie between us was instantly comforting. One of the highlights was watching the boys role-play the delivery-room situation. It was pretty impressive to see how seriously they all took it and how hard they were concentrating, while also being a great source of entertainment for us mothers-to-be. When the course finished on Sunday there were promises of WhatsApp groups and catching up over beers and coffee, and for our group all of those promises came to fruition. We had lucked out, and had met a group of like-minded people who were approaching having a baby in a very similar way to us. It doesn't always happen like that, of course, but the chances are that there'll be a few people at least who you're able to bond with, even if it's for a handful of coffee dates at the very beginning when you really need an understanding ear to bend – and caffeine!

Mums + dads picnic

Although we've met up on many memorable occasions as a group – men, women and babies – it's the friendship that has developed between the seven of us mothers that has been the real success story of that NCT weekend. Our unwavering support for each other has kept us going in our darkest hours when even our own mothers were out of ideas. We have shared everything: tips, anecdotes, the happiest times and the most challenging of times over copious amounts of coffee, a sickening amount of cake and the odd glass of wine. We've both celebrated our little triumphs and sympathised when things were tough. Our constant WhatsApp thread, which documents our journey right from the beginning, has been nothing short of a lifeline and provided comfort and company during those long and lonely nights when our babies were tiny.

It's wonderful how seven strangers have gone on to share and experience the most life-changing event together, and although we were lucky, we are not an oddity; it happens for lots of men and women who find friends for life through NCT.

Little did we know during that weekend in December how significant we would become in each other's lives.

The best part is that we still like each other, even without the babies. Marissa would be the first to agree.

'Ever since the decision was made between my husband and me that we wanted to have a a child together breastfeeding was never ever something I wanted to do. I think the hardest part was attending the NCT class for breastfeeding, I wasn't going to attend but the class leader didn't actually mention that this class was about breastfeeding, so I turned up to a bunch of pictures on the ground of ladies breastfeeding in different situations and we had to pick the one we were drawn to the most. Of course I was drawn to none of them. I was fortunate enough to have enough confidence in myself to announce to the group that actually I was not drawn to any of them and that I would proudly formula feed my baby. My NCT leader was fabulous and while teaching the other ladies different positions for breastfeeding she gladly handed me an empty bottle and gave me tips on how to bottle feed.' Charlotte

LABOUR DAY

'I would rather break my foot repeatedly with a sledge hammer than do that again,' said Laura, 42, and a friend of mine.

Most people are reticent to talk about their experience in great detail, conscious, I suppose, of scaring any mothers-to-be. Plus there's the 'halo effect' where the euphoria of holding your new baby in your arms diminishes the memory of the pain it took to get to that point. Not Laura, though; her experience is obviously still very, very raw. Laura is an oddity, blunt as an old woman's nail scissors, and less maternal than the average bear, and she thought it her duty to be a 'proper' friend and tell me exactly what was in store for me. Thanks for the heads-up.

There are some women who are the polar opposite of Laura and go to great lengths to convince you that they had a 'magical' birth that was 'orgasmic'. Oh please! We all know that in a nutshell, birth involves a female human having to somehow produce another small human from a very tight space, to put it politely, and so the chances of orgasmic are slim at best. If you are one of those rare ones though, good on you.

My birth was somewhere in the middle between excruciating and ecstatic, and on the whole, it was definitely a positive experience. Yep, you don't hear that very often, do you? Of course, it was painful, but so is tonsillitis, and you get nothing at the end of that, just leftover antibiotics. Look, I know that this is the section that lots of mothers-to-be will flick to first, and let me assure you that there will be no scare-mongering here, just the truth and nothing but the truth. Women have been giving birth for millennia, and my story and the others here in many ways are just more for the pile, but you never know, they may just help.

Ready? Deep breath. We're going in.

NESTING

Friday, 20 January 2016. I was 39 weeks pregnant. By this point my maternity leave was in full swing and, contrary to the vision I had conjured up months previously where I would be relaxing on the sofa, cuppa in one hand, biscuit in the other, glued to a Netflix series, I had the mother of all lists to complete and was running around like a headless chicken, dragging my ginormous bump with me. As you know, we had just moved back into our house after a major renovation (that's right, the timing was exceptional) and I was on a mission to empty boxes, sort and nest in that order before the inevitable happened. Despite the fact that my ankles were swollen and the only shoes that would fit my expanding trotters were flip-flops – please note that it was mid-winter – I was determined to carry on regardless. I even fitted in a long walk with a friend and her dog in the afternoon. I was huge, yet I had the energy of a 12-year-old child.

At 7.15pm Charlie, arriving back from work, walked past the window and did a double take as he saw my chubby calves at eye level. Damn it, I had meant to get down off the stepladder where I was filling shelves with books before he got home. The first exchange between us that evening was less than pleasant as he ranted about danger and stupidity, and angrily presented me with a load of other health-and-safety-related facts.

He was right, of course, yet I had this overwhelming need to achieve, to tick everything off the list. I didn't stop until I collapsed, exhausted and, for the first time in my pregnancy, nauseous, in front of Graham Norton. 'Nesting' is an actual instinct in all pregnant mammals, humans included, and is not a term that is just bandied around at NCT classes and in some of the other books that you might read. The need to create a safe and protective environment for the newborn comes on strong and although it is apparently an old wives' tale that once the nesting urge begins, labour is imminent, that 'old wife' was spot on with me, because 12 hours later we were in business.

GOING INTO LABOUR

I wake up to a beautiful, crisp, sunny day. Despite feeling a bit uncomfortable going to bed the night before, I have slept like a log – nine whole hours of undisturbed sleep for the first time in a while. Unbeknownst to me, I am ready for the epic day and night that lies ahead. Isn't the body clever?

Charlie is still fast asleep behind me, so I gently move his arm that lies heavily across my middle and get up quietly to go to the bathroom. As soon as I stand up and pull on my dressing gown, I know that something is happening. A sensation similar to when your period arrives. I make my way slowly across the landing towards the toilet, my instinct telling me that today is the day and, sure enough, my instinct was right. It was show time in more ways than one.

If you're reading this and imagining songs from the musicals and jazz hands, you probably need to up your research, but in the meantime let me enlighten you. In your late pregnancy, the baby will settle down into your pelvis. The sensation is sometimes described as 'lightening' because you'll feel relief from the pressure on your stomach and lungs as the baby moves down. When the baby is engaged, the body responds by producing a hormone that causes the cervix to ripen and shorten in readiness for labour. This in turn causes the mucus plug to dislodge and slip away, creating what is known as the bloody show. Too much? Hang on in there because you ain't seen nothing yet.

I waddle back to bed, a bit unsteady on my feet, mild period cramps kicking in and feeling particularly hot, despite it being mid-January. I whisper to Charlie that things are happening. Still foggy from sleep, it takes him a few seconds to grasp what I'm saying, and then a huge smile spreads across his face. Remembering all the advice we had at our NCT classes about how long labour can take to kick in, we decide to try to relax into it and enjoy tea and a big pile of toast in bed and pretend to concentrate on the seafood linguine that Rick Stein is making on *Saturday Kitchen*.

An hour later, while I'm manically trying to read and digest the whole of *Mindful Birthing*, a book sent to me by my good friend Eleanor the day before, the old, familiar sensation of period pain intensifies, a dull ache spreading from my lower back, around my hips and to the tops of my thighs, tightening around my pelvis in a vice-like grip. It reaches a climax and I throw the book to the floor and get on all fours on the bed, hot, sweaty and feeling faint. Slowly, the pain and sensation subside but I think that I've just experienced my first contraction.

You may assume that from there onwards, things move quickly, but no, there is nothing, not even a twinge, for six hours. It really is a waiting game.

My parents are due to visit from Wales that weekend, and when they ring to say that they are in Swindon, as they always do at the halfway point, I can't resist telling Mum that I have an inkling that baby Thomson is thinking about making an appearance soon.

The hysteria on the other side forces me to pull the phone from my ear.

'Alun! We can't stop for coffee. It's coming, quick! The baby's coming!'

'Hang on, Mum, I think it's going to be a while—'

Ignoring me, 'We'll be with you in an hour!'

When I open the door, fully dressed with the instructions for some flat-pack wardrobes from Ikea in my hand, my mother can't hide her disappointment.

Dad and Charlie set about erecting the wardrobes while Mum washes all the baby clothes and I pack my hospital bag. I know, I know... Everybody told me that I should have done this sooner, but honestly, as long as you have all the bits and pieces that you need, you really don't need to panic. You will know when the deadline is approaching and to be honest, doing it at the last minute will focus the mind and give you something to do while you're waiting for things to progress.

Later that afternoon, I am on my way upstairs with a tray of tea and biscuits for the boys when, out of the blue, my second contraction hits me like a bolt from the blue. This time, there is no denying the intensity. I manage to put the tray down at the top of the stairs before clinging on to the banister for support. I close my eyes and grit my teeth, unable to cry out, just frozen to the spot, paralysed by the sudden onslaught of pain and suddenly very scared by the newness of it. It feels like minutes, but what must only be seconds later, it passes.

'Are you all right, Al?' Mum is at the bottom of the stairs.

'Mmmm,' I manage.

She's smiling as she tells me to sit there for a minute while she gets a glass of water. There's no sign of me when she gets back. I've disappeared into the bathroom.

The poo question

Now, I have a slight phobia of toilet talk. I'm one of those who can't go when I'm on holiday, you know what I mean? I don't want to talk about it, but to give you a clear picture of labour and all it involves, we need to give this subject a bit of airtime.

So, the same hormone that causes the mucus plug to dislodge, prostaglandin, also stimulates your bowels to open more regularly, making way for the baby. I see the bathroom five or six times that afternoon before we leave for the hospital. It's basically like a free colonic and just when you think surely we're done here, it just keeps happening, your body expelling stuff you probably ate back in the late 1990s.

It's not pretty, but at least you know it's normal. Also, there is a lot of paranoia about having a poo during labour – and I admit that it bothered me too – but the good news is that the more you go before, the less likely it is to happen during. However, if it does happen, I can guarantee you that you will not care, plus, midwives have seen it all before and will get rid of the offending article before anybody, least of all you, notices, so it's a huge waste of brain space to worry about it in the lead-up.

Things start moving...

By 4pm, the contractions are now coming more regularly, one every 30 minutes or so, but I know I still have a very long way to go. I feel pretty normal in between, though, and can carry on with various chores. I even try to time my contractions so that I can make a quick dash to the pet shop to buy some treats for our 'other children', Daffy and Kiwi the hamsters, so that they still feel loved while we're at hospital. I know, I know... what was I thinking? Mum tries her best to convince me that this is a bad idea and she is right. You see, my timings were a bit off, and I scared the guinea pigs half to death as I gripped the side of their cage and pressed my face against the cool metal, teeth bared, while riding out another contraction in the middle of the pet shop. It must have been a terrifying couple of minutes for those poor small animals and every other customer in the shop. It was a pretty traumatic experience all round, but these days, I get ten per cent off there though so every cloud...

The much-talked-about birth plan

During your last few appointments, your midwife will advise you to write a birth plan and while I recognise that it's helpful for you and your partner to have a good chat about various aspects of the birth and decide on some of the basics, like whether you'd favour the traditional labour ward or a birth centre, what pain relief, if any, you would be up for having, who should cut the cord, etc., I would really encourage you to be as fluid and as flexible as you possibly can. Too many of my friends had completely overthought it and were disappointed when things didn't go to plan and panicked when they found themselves in a situation that was different to what they had imagined. Try to avoid that. It will be what it will be. Labour is one scenario that even the most OCD among us cannot meticulously plan for.

We were completely fluid. Well, to be honest, we forgot to write a birth plan. We also forgot to buy a TENS machine and forgot to go to hypnobirthing classes, but hey-ho. In a nutshell, my game plan was simply to avoid going to the hospital for as long as possible and then to just see what happened.

'Hypnobirthing. It sounds lovely; breathe the pain away, control, strength, inner strength and listening to your body... Luckily my experience birthing my first child was all of the above. I'd go as far as saying it was magical, empowering, it made me a strong woman. My baby boy arrived at 8pm, no medication, no screaming, no fear. It was truly a birth without fear. Yes it still bloody hurt at times but it was so calm and controlled; it was life-changing for so many reasons. Second time around...

41 weeks pregnant with my daughter, I decided hypnobirthing wasn't for her. I put my three-year-old son to bed, I felt sick, I had period pain type aches … 45 minutes later she arrived on the front room floor delivered by my neighbour! I strongly encourage my friends not to make birth plans, go with the flow. What will happen will happen, listen to your body and trust the medical staff. We are strong.' Aimee

Time for the hospital

At 8.20pm, with me hanging on to Charlie's back as another strenuous contraction rips through me, I know it's time to throw in the towel and get to the hospital. Mum and Dad are casually tucking into some spaghetti bolognese while they time my contractions, the heady waft of beef and red wine making me want to vomit. Once we hit one minute and 30 seconds between each one, Mum authoritatively announces that enough is enough and that she is going to bloody well drive us there herself unless we leave that very moment.

Begrudgingly, I pull on some biker boots that go beautifully with the tracksuit bottoms I'm wearing, fling on a huge coat and get in the car while Charlie grabs my hospital bag. Mum and Dad, having kissed us goodbye and wished us luck, stand at the door waving, and just as Charlie reaches for the door handle on the driver's side, our neighbour appears with a parcel for us that had been delivered to them by mistake. While I am dealing with an in-car contraction that is exactly as you see in the films (two hands on the ceiling and bum off the seat, writhing in agony) Charlie is on the pavement listening to some pure nonsense about how the delivery man had gone to the wrong address because our front door is on a different street to the street on the envelope, blah, blah, blah... Instead of telling our neighbour that his wife is in labour and that we really need to crack on, Charlie stands there manically nodding, politely willing the most pointless story ever to end. The exchange between us on the way to the Queen Charlotte hospital is frosty. I am very close to being a new mum with a murder conviction.

Charlie offers to drop me off at the door while he finds a parking spot, but in my wisdom I refuse and say I'll be fine to walk from the car park. I just don't want to go in on my own. This is a mistake. The walk, which should take seven minutes, is closer to 30 as I hold on steadfastly to railings, cars and even other humans while navigating the strongest contractions yet.

'Straight up to the first floor, love,' says a kind-looking nurse who is standing in reception. Around the corner there are three lifts that seemingly all take their passengers on the same journey. However, that wasn't the case. In a true *Sliding Doors*-esque moment, and completely unbeknownst to me, I chose the lift that took us to the birth centre, securing myself a natural, drug-free delivery in a touch of a button.

The birth centre

I mean, I had considered the birth centre, I'd done the tour and, in theory, liked the ethos behind it, but I had been reluctant to fully commit for two reasons. The first was the obvious lack of any pain-relief drugs, including the much-hailed epidural. Secondly, I worried about the possibilities of suffering complications due to my 'primigravida' age and there being no actual doctors there to deal with them.

However, my fate is sealed but I don't concede without a fight.

'I really don't want to be here,' I wail pathetically as I take off my trousers so that Nia, the midwife, can examine me. 'I need to move to the labour ward!'

'OK, just take a deep breath and let me have a look at you and then we'll go from there shall we?' Nia patiently answers. She already knows that I will stay, but that I just need to be talked down from the ledge.

Another contraction takes the wind from my sails and I lie on the bed, bucking like a bronco, knuckles white as I grip the plastic sides of the examination table.

'You're already six centimetres.'

The pain was so severe that I hadn't even realised that I was being examined.

'You can do this, Alex, you're over halfway,' encourages Nia. 'Let me take you through to one of our delivery rooms.'

In a very small window between contractions that are pretty much coming every 60 seconds now, we are shown through to one of the delivery suites in the birth centre. Picture a room that's 20 per cent posher than a Premier Inn bedroom and that is pretty much spot on. As far as its particulars go... Wardrobes on one wall, including one that houses a pull-down double bed, a big whirlpool bath thing for water births in the corner, a huge bean bag that became my lifeline, a separate bathroom and a cot and changing mat for the new arrival. There's also a docking station for your chosen birth playlist (it won't surprise you that we didn't have one of these either) and some of those plastic candles that look a bit nasty close up but create a nice enough effect, and truth be told, lighting is everything in this situation.

It's Charlie's turn to nest now. He sets about emptying my case, methodically lining up our drinks and snacks, putting my toilet bag in the bathroom, looking for appropriate music on his phone, basically keeping himself busy while I move like a female gorilla from one end of the room to the other, making deep guttural noises and contemplating the insurmountable task that lies ahead.

Suddenly there's a knock on the door. It's the midwife asking whether my parents are with us. No. We had said goodbye and left them at the house. 'Oh OK, that's weird,' says Nia, 'because there's a Welsh-speaking couple in the waiting room.'

Of course they've followed us. They can't help themselves, and now that I'm a parent myself I completely understand why they wanted to be there. The next half an hour is like an episode of *Gavin and Stacey* as Mum and Dad come to say a 'quick hello'. I am leaning on the side of the birthing pool, breathing very loudly. I have entered the animalistic phase, which must be especially weird for Dad to see, and so he busies himself by hanging our coats up in the wardrobe while Mum puts the kettle on. To be fair, they quickly realise that four is a crowd and retreat to the waiting room, where they wait with bated breath for 12 whole hours, taking it in turns to grab short naps on the hard, unwelcoming benches like only parents can.

The birth centre isn't some posh private wing, it's available to all on the NHS and offers a peaceful, spacious and calming environment, the antithesis of the strip-lit, chaotic and noise-filled labour ward. There are no doctors, but plenty of very experienced and brilliant midwives who are always on hand, but their approach is to give you and your partner space until the prep work is done and it's time to push. Each birth centre varies and not all offer a birthing pool; but this is the main reason why some women choose this path so when the hospital offers you a tour of their labour facilities, be sure to take it so that you know exactly what to expect.

Some might find the lack of involvement from the midwives strange, but after an hour or so, Charlie and I are hitting our stride. Active labour is in full swing and I am on all fours on the bean bag as all the pain is in my back, and Charlie sits on a chair facing me. I signal to him that another contraction is building and, just as we had learnt at our NCT classes, he quietly talks me through it and breathes with me until the pain becomes manageable again. There is no screaming or cursing, just synchronised breathing and deep concentration. We stay in this exact position for five hours. It is intense and brutal, yet beautiful at

6cm dilated + thinking the world war ending

the same time, as we work together to bring our child into the world. Charlie's support, and the manner in which he takes complete control of the situation, makes me fall in love with him over and over again that night.

BREAKING THE WATERS

One of the biggest misconceptions I had about labour was that unless I was overdue, my waters breaking would be the first sign that labour had started. In reality, only ten per cent of women will experience their waters breaking before contractions have started. Shame I hadn't read that statistic before Charlie and I had slept for a fortnight on an unsexy, crunchy, wipe-clean sheet in anticipation. I am in full-on established labour, contractions flooring me one after another, when, out of nowhere, my waters break with a very loud pop. It is exactly like feeling a balloon burst inside me. From there, things step up a gear.

> 'My husband John and I were having our final holiday together in the Algarve. I was 27 weeks pregnant and feeling great, until going into what I didn't realise was early labour. After some time, we were taken by ambulance to the local hospital. I was checked over and hit with the devastating news that my baby was going to be born within the next few hours. I was so shocked. I remember the pain of the contractions, while waiting for the NICU team from Faro hospital to turn up. I asked for pain relief, but was refused as they believed that might damage the baby. About four hours later, I gave birth naturally to a beautiful but tiny 2lb 4oz baby boy. He cried when he was born, which made me realise his strength. After a few stitches as

I was bleeding fairly heavily, I was wheeled in to see him before his journey to Faro. I was then wheeled into a room where a curtain separated me from someone else who had given birth. She got to keep her baby, and that's when I completely lost it. I broke down and was in a complete state. The doctor offered me a sedative but I refused. I spent the night in another room with two very young, heavily pregnant women who were kind despite the language barrier.. John and I were told that the staff would do their best to save our baby's life. The walls of NICU, wires, monitors etc became our world for 84 days. The first month was hell. Having a daily fight with Mike Tyson would have been easier. Our baby had numerous issues, infections, lumbar punctures, breathing issues, cow's protein allergy. It was intense and difficult. The most problematic was a large brain bleed and suspected hydrocephalus. Fortunately, this resolved by itself, and he did not require surgery. Patrick was two in October, and despite such a tough start he is doing remarkably well.' Rachel

Water baby

I never thought that I would want to get into the birthing pool. Never, ever. I'd heard a million women enthuse about the pool, many citing a water birth as their ideal labour, but I didn't think it was for me. One, I'm not a huge fan of water and two, it meant completely stripping off, and even in this situation, being naked was something I was loathe to do, even though I knew that there was no way our baby was being born while I still had tracksuit bottoms on.

However, just like everyone says, dignity is left on the bathroom floor along with the saturated tracksuit bottoms from my waters breaking and, with just a bra to cover my modesty, in I get. Normally, I have strong opinions about wearing a bra and no knickers; it feels so wrong and looks offensive – but I am way past caring at this point. To be honest, by the time I am eight centimetres dilated, I am ready to give anything a go: water pool, jumping out of the window... you get the picture. Despite my scepticism, the warm water feels wonderful, especially in the absence of any hard-core pain relief, and I would highly recommend it.

There I am, on my knees, chin resting on the side of the pool, the gas and air tube between my teeth, eyes closed. The sheer physicality of the last few hours has exhausted me. We stay like that for 30 minutes or so, silent and calm in the dimly lit suite, with only the contractions, which are further apart now occasionally, rousing me from a dream-like state. I have reached what they call the 'transitional phase', and as the contractions lessen, the urge to bear down and push comes on strong. I'm really terrified now. I've only just got used to the contractions, but this brand-new sensation is confirmation that he or she is really on their way and pushing is the only option. I feel completely out of my depth. Charlie, sensing my fear, calls Mum into the room.

'I'm really scared, Mum,' I whisper as she takes my hand.

'Shhh.' She strokes my damp hair. 'You're doing really well, Al, you're nearly there.'

Another examination confirms that I have reached the magic ten centimetres and am ready to push. Your instinct completely takes over now, and all you can do is try to summon enough energy to keep up with the demands that your body is putting on you. There are two midwives in the room as the

clock strikes 5am, scrubbed up and ready to safely guide baby
Thomson out into the world.

Time to push

I lie on my side on the bean bag and start the long road to
delivery. The first half an hour is futile. The urge to push is
exactly like wanting to go to the toilet, and instead of doing
as the midwives encourage and going with it, I find myself
unable to, scared of the outcome and doing everything to go
against the pull of gravity. Gently, they move me to a birthing
stool, an attractive piece of kit reminiscent of the Victorian
era. With Charlie perched behind me, and the midwives at my
feet, the real labour starts in earnest. Each contraction forces
you to push, and with each wave I managed about four. I was
falling asleep in between each round and, despite Charlie's best
efforts to keep my energy up by feeding me liquorice bars, I
couldn't swallow as my mouth was too dry from the gas and air,
even though I must have gone through litres of water. By this
stage, it's decided that the Entonox is actually halting progress
and, like ripping someone's right arm off, it was wheeled away
and out of sight.

> 'It's important women should be open and honest about
> childbirth and motherhood with zero judgement! After a
> miscarriage at three months with my first, I had extreme
> anxiety in my pregnancy, which led me to yoga and
> hypnobirthing. Both of which were a godsend. My waters
> broke at 36 weeks, and my little girl Luna was born at
> 36 plus two days. I was induced by the drip. I used a
> hypnobirthing app... listened to it every time I was in

> the bath and on my walk into work each day. In labour, even though the situation with early baby was out of my control, I felt my mind was calmed and focused, almost "elsewhere". I felt in awe of my body and the strength of the contractions was something bigger than myself (?!!!) I found it was such an empowering experience and I feel proud. Proud that I grew this teeny 5lb 11oz bubs and brought her into the world.' Sadie

Then there is nothing, just my body working harder than it ever has before. It's excruciating, ruthless and animalistic, but it's eye-on-the-prize time. Crowning is by far the most painful sensation. 'Ring of fire' is often used to describe it. To be fair, it's pretty accurate, but add a serious dose of Tabasco for the full picture. A look in a mirror gives us our first glance of the top of our baby's head... a mop of dark hair, and suddenly I have to have him all.

Wide awake for the first time in hours, and with maternal adrenalin pumping through my veins, I push like I could move a mountain. My other focus is to be as silent as I possibly can, hoping that this will translate as a less traumatic birth for Teddy. Charlie still swears that I didn't curse or shout. It's funny how my maternal instinct kicks in and gives me the strength to see this through and I honestly think that Ted has the lovely laid-back temperament that he does because of that quiet and measured entrance into the world.

We are parents...

It is 7.19am on 22 January 2017 and ten months of worry and questions are put to bed. Charlie kisses me on the forehead and says, 'Meet your little boy' as he proudly places my brand-new son in my arms. These next few minutes will always be the best moments of my life. With my baby tucked into my chest, I feel more at peace than I ever have before. I look up at Charlie, who smiles back, and without any words we know that we are the happiest we've ever been. Gently kissing the top of my little boy's head, I know with instant clarity that nothing else will ever matter as much, and for the first time, I really know who I am and what my purpose is.

> 'While I was pregnant the only thing that worried me about having a baby was the medical side – hospitals, needles, epidurals, catheters.... so I decided a home birth would be the best option. When I went into labour I felt totally prepared, I knew what my body was doing and the hypnobirthing techniques combined with what I'd learnt in yoga allowed me to have a completely calm birth, no drugs, no gas and air, just breathing. I felt like I was in my own little bubble and that I'd slept through most of it. This was despite a hospital transfer from home and an episiotomy!' Abbie

THE AFTERMATH...

I knew that delivering the placenta would disturb our love-in, and it did in the most unimaginable way. Delivering the placenta is known as the third stage of labour, but like most mothers, I assumed that the hard work was done and dusted. I accepted the midwife's offer of an injection to speed up the delivery and no sooner than the empty vessel had been thrown in the waste bin, my body expelled the placenta and with it came a huge gush of blood. Teddy was still lying in my arms, both of us happily drinking in each other's features, firmly on cloud nine, but one look at the ashen face of Charlie, who had just witnessed the tsunami of blood, told me that we were in trouble. Gone were the drunk-in-love eyes, his jaw was tight and his brow furrowed. In a blink of an eye – our serene environment became chaotic, two midwives became six, joy turned to panic.

The downside of the birthing centre, as mentioned, was that there weren't any doctors on hand to deal with what was, unbeknownst to me, an emergency. My uterus had failed to contract due to the fact that the placenta had left the building at such speed, resulting in life-threatening blood loss. I was trolleyed up to the next floor, past my parents, who didn't even know what sex their new grandchild was yet, and into the brightly lit emergency room where a seven-strong medical team were waiting. There were stitches, cannulas being inserted and lots of shouting. With my legs in stirrups, I stared helplessly at Charlie, who stood on the sidelines, his face etched with concern, holding our brand-new baby wrapped in just a towel that had been grabbed in haste as we left the delivery suite.

The brilliant team at the Queen Charlotte were, thankfully, very quick to get the situation under control and, although it was utterly traumatic for Charlie and my parents, I was oblivious to what exactly was going on. Having my baby back in my arms put the horrendous past hour firmly to the back of my mind. It affected Charlie the most; at the worst point, he was left to contemplate life as a single dad. It's well documented how tough labour is for the woman, but by 10am on that

Sunday, Charlie had also been through the hardest 12 hours of his life.

With visiting over, Charlie sneaked into my bed and there we lay with Teddy on his chest. We just looked at him in awe, amazed at his tiny hands, his fingers, his button nose, and obsessed with sniffing his little head. It sounds bizarre, but it really is the best smell in the world and it's the one smell I wish I could bottle forever. With our eyes getting heavy, we placed a sleepy Teddy in the crib next to the bed and fell into a deep and content sleep. The first of many as a family of three.

Exhausted but elated. Ted is our world!

CHOOSING
A PLACE TO GIVE BIRTH
NIA WILLIAMS, MY MIDWIFE

HOME BIRTH

▷ Recommended for women who are low-risk medically and have an uncomplicated pregnancy.

▷ Two midwives attend your home and support you through labour and giving birth – either NHS midwives from your local hospital or you can choose to hire private independent midwives.

▷ Giving birth at home is just as safe as having a hospital birth if it is your second or subsequent baby. If it is your first baby, home birth is slightly less safe than a hospital birth.

▷ Choose a home birth if it is important to you to:
- labour and give birth in familiar and private surroundings;
- have the freedom to choose which of your loved ones are present at your birth (in hospital, you may be limited to a maximum of two support partners);
- move freely during labour, have an active birth;
- give birth with the least amount of intervention;
- avoid pharmaceutical analgesi.

> 'I was terrified of labour – I'd never really had much of a pain threshold! But in the end, what they all say turned out to be true – your body really does just *know* what to do, it completely takes over.' Holly

BIRTH CENTRE

▷ Recommended for women who are low-risk medically and have an uncomplicated pregnancy.

▷ Midwives working in a birth centre are experts in normal birth.

▷ Giving birth in a birth centre is as safe as an obstetric unit for women having their first baby.

▷ Choose a birth centre if it is important to you to:

- give birth in a home-from-home environment;
- move freely during labour, have an active birth;
- use water during labour and birth;
- give birth with the least amount of intervention;
- avoid pharmaceutical analgesia (most birth centres have gas and air available).

OBSTETRIC UNIT

▷ Recommended for women who have a medical condition that makes them high-risk or have a complicated pregnancy.

▷ Midwives working on obstetric units are experts in caring for high-risk women and work closely alongside doctors.

▷ Choose an obstetric unit if it is important to you to:

- have access to an epidural;
- have medical backup close at hand (although, in most birth centres, medical backup is quickly accessible in an emergency).

TIPS FOR LABOUR
NIA WILLIAMS, MY MIDWIFE
Head midwife at the birthing centre
in the Queen Charlotte Hospital West London

◇ **Attend birth preparation classes** and take your birth support partner with you. Fear of the unknown leads to unnecessary stress, which can slow down the progress of labour.

◇ Tell friends and family that you are only interested in hearing **positive birth stories**.

◇ Consider **backup labour support** but ensure they have a positive and relaxed attitude to birth. Some couples choose to hire a doula to support, guide and act as an advocate through their labour and birth.

◇ **Imagine the course of labour** as a hill, its peak being strong, regular contractions and a cervical dilation of 4cms (the medical definition of established labour). The incline to the peak (referred to as latent or early labour) can be a slow and challenging climb. If you reach this point in good condition, your journey to full dilation and baby in your arms is likely to be quicker. If you arrive at hospital after the peak, you are far less likely to require medical intervention.

◇ **Approach labour as if you are doing a marathon**. The uterus is a large muscle that needs a steady supply of energy to contract.

◇ Consume **slow-energy-release foods** such as pasta, rice, porridge and wholemeal toast in early labour in order to keep your blood sugar stable. Save high-sugar foods such as cereal bars, dried fruit and chocolate for established labour (i.e. hospital) when you need a quick energy-boosting snack.

◇ Starving yourself in labour can lead to irregular, ineffective contractions with the potential of prolonging labour and ultimately increasing the risk of unnecessary intervention.

◇ **Rest!** As much as you can in the early stages, while the contractions are spaced. There will come a point where they are close enough that you find it much harder to rest in between but you may still be in early labour at this point. Warm baths can help you to relax.

◇ **Distraction**. A great strategy for early labour – go and watch that film you've been meaning to get to, go out for lunch, take a walk in the park. Enjoy those last few moments as a couple!

◇ Avoid timing your contractions until you feel they're coming close together (one every five minutes or less).

◇ Many women value the use of **hypnobirthing** during their labour and birth, a technique incorporating meditative practice, visualisation and positive affirmation. There are numerous hypnobirthing practitioners in the UK who can be easily found via the internet.

◇ If a **voice within** is telling you to go to the hospital, listen to it.

◇ Once at hospital, **remain upright** and as mobile as possible; gravity helps the cervix to dilate and brings baby down into a good position for birth.

◇ If you identify a **fear of labour and birth** during your pregnancy that you believe might be more than the usual nerves or is preventing you from enjoying your pregnancy, speak to your midwife/GP as soon as possible; there is support available to you. You have a right to enjoy this special time and look forward to welcoming your baby.

◇ Most importantly, believe in your ability to birth your baby – **you are amazing**.

PART
—
2

LIFE
AFTER

WELCOME TO THE CLUB.
THE FIRST FEW MONTHS IN THE
WILDERNESS!

THE
TOP 5
MOST ANNOYING
THINGS

YOU MIGHT HEAR IN THE FIRST FEW MONTHS*
*and must just ignore

1. I found breastfeeding a dream, it came so naturally to me

2. I find it's easier to get the housework done before 9am

3. Mine slept through the night from the word go

4. I'll say this about younger parents – they do seem to have more energy

5. My body just bounced back!

ALL THE GEAR, NO IDEA!

On a particularly bitter January afternoon, two days after I'd given birth, we wrapped tiny Ted in as many layers as we feasibly could and prepared to leave our cocoon at the Queen Charlotte hospital, bracing ourselves for what lay ahead. We bid an emotional farewell to the midwives who had cared for us so tenderly and made everything feel manageable. The extended stay at the hospital, due to the complications at the end of my labour, had been a godsend and really cushioned our fall into parenthood.

So there we were ecstatic and high on adrenalin, swooshing confidently through the double doors, Teddy in the car seat, we swapped the stuffy warmth of the hospital for the fresh January afternoon as we stepped into our brand-new life as a family.

After double- and triple-checking that the car seat was properly secured into the iso-fix, Charlie's OCD already kicking up a notch in his new role as dad, we set off for home confident and optimistic, Charlie driving and me in the back next to Teddy.

Our optimism lasted all of three minutes. By the time we'd pulled out of the junction and could see the hospital shrinking through the back window, I was in tears. It started small and grew into loud, uncontrollable sobs. Charlie looked at me in the rear-view mirror, his face etched with concern, but I just couldn't articulate what was wrong. I suppose it was a combination of things – on the one hand I felt nostalgic about those past few days that we had shared in the hospital where our life had changed forever, and I also felt racked with nerves about how we would handle the huge challenge and change that lay ahead. It suddenly felt very real.

Teddy seemed to sense my fear and started wailing. We'd hardly heard a peep from him during our 48-hour stay in hospital and had proudly commented on 'what a good baby' he was that practically slept all the time. This, of course, is a very common mistake that tons of first-time parents make. The shock of the January chill had properly roused him, and his delicate, shrill cries filled the car; a sound I'll never forget because it sounded like he was saying 'Allah' over and over again. He might well have been praying for us all.

We were lucky to have the tour de force that is my mother to welcome us home from the hospital, making sure that everything was sorted, the heating was cranked up and all the baby equipment was good to go as soon as we walked through the door. She was our lifeline for the first couple of weeks – but ultimately, my parents live too far away to be on hand to help constantly, so we had no choice but to work it out between us.

THE FIRST MONTHS

I won't lie to you, the first three to six weeks are brutal. Wonderful in so many ways, but brutal. Just when you think that you've got life sussed and sorted, having a baby can make you feel totally incompetent. It really doesn't matter how many books you've read or how many antenatal classes you attend, practical parenting is challenging and, sometimes, a complete head wreck. All you can do is strap yourself in, hold on tightly and go with the flow as much as you can, knowing that eventually you will come out on the other side.

The truth is, that being a first time older parent means that you are already at an advantage in many ways. Oh, yes, there are plenty of upsides to starting out on the family front in your 30's and 40's. For example you'll have more patience and tolerance, virtues that you will need by the bucket load, not just for the baby, but for each other. You're likely to have developed a good dose of common sense, which will get you through most tricky situations that you're presented with. Also, the likelihood is that by the time you've reached your mid-thirties you will have a nicer house to bring your child home to than you would have had a decade ago. You will have better incomes to be able to afford the endless paraphernalia that you need for a baby and so all the vital equipment will be at your fingertips. You will just be set up and braced for the challenge ahead in a way that wouldn't have been as possible in your twenties.

PATERNITY LEAVE

Charlie opted to split his two-week statutory paternity leave into two separate weeks so that he could have the first week with us, and take the remaining week when his mother came to visit from New Zealand. It was fleeting, but that first week, when it was the three of us getting to know each other, remains the most special of all. It was mid-winter and so we hunkered down. Teddy slept for most of it and, despite the trials and tribulations of feeding, we managed to snuggle up on the sofa and watch the odd film! It was heaven.

After that, the balance shifted and I was home alone with Ted. On bad days, I would resent the fact that Charlie got himself suited and booted and off to work while I lay in stained jogging bottoms and a maternity bra trying clumsily to get Teddy to latch on to my swollen boobs to feed. I would hear the front door slam, the smell of his aftershave lingering in the air long after he'd hurriedly kissed us both goodbye, and I would lie there in a daze trying to grasp this new set-up. We were used to leading equally busy working lives, but biology had put a temporary hold on that, and we were right back in hunter-gatherer times, which I struggled with. It's tough on both parents though, because on the other hand Charlie would despair at leaving for a 12-hour shift at the office, worrying that his long absences would interfere in his bonding with his new son. If only we lived in Sweden, where paternity leave had recently been extended to three months. The Scandis really do have it all worked out when it comes to parenting.

> 'I worry that my son will bond stronger with my wife because she's always there for him during the days. Does he understand that I don't just disappear because I don't care? There's a lot of guilt and worry in my mind. But then I get moments of such peace when I see my happy little family, or when my son smiles at me. I feel like the richest, luckiest man in the world.' Richard

SLEEP, FEED, POO, REPEAT

Now, they say that all a baby does in that first period is sleep, feed and poo, which is true; and it sounds simple, but those three elements also bring with them a world of anguish. Nobody tells you how the lack of sleep that you are about to experience will knock you for six, how dealing with that while your body is also recovering from the savageness of labour is the hardest thing you will ever do and how the anxiety of being a new parent will overcome you both. I guarantee that you will spend many hours leaning over the Moses basket listening to your baby breathe and google 'Is my baby's breathing normal?' and then find out that they are doing what is known as periodic breathing, which means that your baby may pause for up to ten seconds between each breath, which obviously, pre-google, meant that you are rendered a nervous wreck!

You will discuss your baby's urine and poo, especially the colour and texture of it, at length, and fret about how runny, mustardy or grainy it is. Then, feeding will bring its own anxiety and complications, based largely around how often you should feed, and how much milk your baby should be drinking. How do you know how much the baby's actually getting when it's coming from your boob and should you wake a sleeping baby to feed it? (It's tempting not to, but you probably should, especially in those first few weeks).

'My partner suffered with hyperemesis gravidarum (severe sickness throughout the whole pregnancy). She has also suffered from anxiety, specifically health anxiety. She was in hospital three times during her pregnancy due to the sickness and several more due to what she thought were reduced movements. The anxiety led her to believe her not being able to eat was affecting the baby. She had to miss out on breastfeeding due to a skin condition, so I stepped up and told Amy I would do all of the night feeds and stuck to it for nine months while working full time. This allowed my partner to recover from the terrible pregnancy both physically and mentally, while allowing me a great opportunity to bond with my son (and get some brownie points on board as well!).' Maya

THIS TOO SHALL PASS...

The dense fog of the first three months will eventually lift, and although the days can seem long and the nights even longer, have confidence in yourselves because you've absolutely got this and you *will* work it out.

I don't feel that I need to include all the really basic info in here. As I said, this book isn't a manual; you're more than capable of accessing the basics via the good old internet if need be, plus you still have your midwife to turn to in the first few weeks after labour. This chapter is more of a support group in book form.

You've waited a long time for this life changer, so try your best to embrace every moment from the very high highs, to the lowest of the lows and everything in between. Everybody's experience will be unique but the struggles will be similar. All you can do is give it your best shot and in return you'll feel love like you've never felt before. 'Winging it' starts here.

TEMPORARY TRAIN WRECK

Before we start talking about the baby, I want to talk about you.

As a parent, you are already amazing. You've brought your little boy or girl into the world and that in itself is a huge feat. Throughout my pregnancy, I was shocked at how little advice was available about recovery after labour. Not a single midwife mentioned it. I assumed that my post-partum self wouldn't be pretty, but nothing could prepare me for the wreckage I was left with and how much healing it really took before I felt human again. To the outside world, I probably looked OK relatively quickly, but underneath my clothes was a very different story.

I was in the shower, six days after giving birth, and tentatively tried just one pelvic floor exercise. Just one.

Nothing. Not even a twitch. It was as if my top half was completely disconnected from my bottom half, as if the anaesthetic from the stitches still hadn't worn off. I panicked and started manically googling 'is vaginal numbness normal?' Followed by 'is vaginal recovery slower for 35+?'

Once your baby arrives, he or she will be the sole focus of attention and nobody, not even your own mother or midwife, cares that your body feels and looks like it's been through a devastating war. The only question that the midwife will ask is whether you've managed to 'empty your bowels yet'. This is something I put off for as long as possible, convinced that my entire insides would fall heavily into the toilet bowl at the slightest chance of exit. The truth was that while it's uncomfortable, it's just best to get it over with. The thought of it is worse than the reality.

The post-partum experience is different for everyone. 'Post-partum', let's just mull that word over for a sec, say it to yourself... P.O.S.T.P.A.R.T.U.M. I don't like the word. Post-parting. That's putting it mildly, I'm afraid. 'Post-ripped-in-halfum' is more accurate.

Don't panic, though. As you may have already read, my birth was actually OK, good even, as much as birthing a human can be, and my recovery, in hindsight, despite my being 39, was quick-ish. Everybody's different though, and there are many factors to consider, such as whether the birth was natural or a C-section, whether labour was straightforward or an emergency situation and, of course, the age of the mother, which contradicts what I just said, but on the whole, the truth is that the body of an average 25-year-old is going to recover quicker than your average 40-year-old – although, like everything, there are always exceptions.

HERE COME THE TEARS...

So, after another sleepless night of excruciating feeding, Mum suggested that I went off to have a shower while she held the fort. It was the best thing she could have said. I felt broken and exhausted and I needed some space just for me. I handed Teddy to Mum and locked the door of the bathroom. The relief at being alone and free from a demanding newborn just for ten minutes was heaven. I ran the shower, the noise drowning out Teddy's cries, and slumped down behind the door, lacking the energy to even pull off my pyjamas. That was the first time I gave in to the emotional rollercoaster that had been the last week and let fat, salty tears roll down my cheeks. I felt overwhelmed, out of my depth and scared that this little human was going to be reliant on me for the rest of my, and his, life. There was no going back to my old life, this was it until he was 18 at best, and I couldn't see the wood for the trees.

THE BABY BLUES
Clemmie Hooper, midwife

It is reported that up to 70 per cent of women experience symptoms of the baby blues within the first weeks of giving birth; it's no surprise considering how much your hormones are changing. The first sign of the 'blues' is often when your milk starts coming in, around day four or five after giving birth (although this differs for everyone). This is when a huge change in your hormones occurs and can trigger feeling weepy, bursting into tears for no reason and feeling irritable, tired and anxious. Having a baby and becoming a mother is a huge deal and feeling overwhelmed by

> this tiny new human who is entirely dependent on you is normal. These feelings don't usually last very long and you'll soon feel a bit more like you again but always speak to your partner/midwife/health visitor if these feelings don't go away.

It's hard to relive those memories now, and I can't believe how long ago it feels, but if I close my eyes I can vividly recall those feelings of despair and fear. At its worst, the self-doubt that consumed me lasted maybe three or four days, but as a 39-year-old woman who was used to being in control and on top of things, this was alien. How could I be successful in many areas of my life yet be crap at the one thing that mattered the most? I couldn't even talk about it. I normally wear my heart on my sleeve, but I couldn't vocalise how disappointed I was at how the first days of motherhood were panning out. I assumed that these feelings would plague younger, less experienced girls, but making that generalisation was stupid and naive of me. Just because I had more miles on the clock didn't automatically mean that I would be a capable parent. That is the thing with becoming a mother; whether you are still a teenager, a career woman in her forties or indeed the Duchess of Cambridge, it's a leveller.

I wasn't coping and – for the first time ever – my body wasn't co-operating. Breastfeeding was proving impossible and my usual plentiful energy stores were drained. As easy as I'd found my pregnancy, giving birth was an acute reminder that I was 39, not 29, and I have little doubt that the extra decade was making my recovery slower, the night feeds more gruelling and the backache, from constantly lifting Teddy and bending to change his nappy, more severe.

'Our first night at home was a nightmare. From 10pm–5am the baby would not stop crying unless she was on my boob. I was convinced something was wrong. I was there with my much wanted daughter, with tears rolling down my cheeks – this was not what I thought it would be like. My husband tried to stay awake to support me but kept falling asleep – I felt so alone. By 7am I'd rung the maternity and told them to send the midwives round ASAP. They turned up at 9am. I was exhausted, in pain and sliding into depression. I didn't want to feed her, I didn't want her near me. I couldn't believe I felt this way. It was my mother who saw what was happening. She said I looked dead behind the eyes, like a ghost. I broke down and she told me there and then to stop. I felt like I was letting everyone down, my daughter, my husband, that I was a failure because I couldn't do this one thing that was supposed to be so natural!' Krysia

I eventually summoned the energy to strip off ready for the shower and took a long, hard look at myself in the mirror for the first time since becoming a mother. I hardly recognised the woman staring back at me. I scanned myself slowly, head to toe. My eyes were small and bloodshot, my lips cracked and dry, set off beautifully by my grey, sallow complexion. Casting my eyes downwards, I saw a pair of ginormous boobs that looked like they belonged to somebody else. They were veiny, at bursting point and hot to the touch. My milk had come in a few days ago and they were unbelievably painful, like carrying around two heavy balls of molten rock. Further down was my loose, empty pouch, looking sad and bereft of the little bundle that it had carried so carefully. It was still swollen, of course, and from the side, there was more than a passing resemblance to Mr Greedy. The skin was slack like a melted candle and hung pathetically. Moving on down and there was more good news. A pair of swollen ankles, like those poor old ladies with terrible water retention who you see pushing their trolleys slowly around the supermarket. My feet matched my ankles. They were full and smooth and looked like they belonged to another person. The icing on the cake was the few grey hairs that sprang from my crown, wiry and conspicuous. I got in the shower and let tears wash over me afresh as I unsuccessfully tried to hand express some milk to relieve my breasts. It was impossible. I gave up and stood there, in a useless daze, warm water washing over me, never wanting to leave the cubicle.

Mum's gentle knock on the bathroom door made me jump. 'Are you OK, Al?' I must have been in there for ages. Teddy was screaming and needed feeding, so reluctantly I turned off the water and started to dry myself. Even that was painful. The soft towel was like a cheese grater over my ravaged nipples and then I became aware of a dull ache, a muscular pain in my nether regions. That lasted for about a fortnight and was sometimes so bad that it would stop me in my tracks and I'd have to steady myself and breathe deeply. The only thing I can compare it to is braking too heavily on your bike when you were little and banging your bits on the bar. Paracetamol and Ibuprofen became my friends and got me through those hellish first few weeks of feeding and healing.

REMEMBER HOW AMAZING YOUR BODY IS. This was a small and temporary blip in hindsight. The feeling on good days was gratitude for what my body has been able to achieve.

I'm still in awe of my body and all it's accomplished. My boobs will never look the same, and I suppose that my skin will always be a little bit saggy around my belly, but I genuinely see them as badges of honour. It would be a lie to say that I prefer my body now to how it was before, but bringing me Teddy was a miracle and I'm grateful for it every day. However, it's fair to say that there was a dip at the very beginning, but don't despair; after much googling I found that those feelings were common and very normal at that stage post-birth so don't panic if you feel the same, but like Clemmie says, seek help if it lasts for more than a few days because, for some, post natal depression becomes a bigger issue.

'When he was born I felt numb towards him and for the first eight weeks of his life masked how I was feeling until I eventually broke down on my husband and admitted all my feelings. That I didn't feel bonded to him and feel that I loved him. Every time he would cry I would fill with dread as I would have to sort him out whether it was a clean nappy, food or just a cuddle. I got diagnosed with post natal anxiety and depression and I'm pleased to say that we are on the road to recovery and my baby and I have a lovely relationship going on.' Jess

THE EARLY WEEKS AND EXERCISE

Before Ted, I used to be active and fit and I assumed that after Ted I would continue in the same vein. How completely deluded was I? On a sunny Saturday morning, seven weeks post-partum and with my fortieth birthday just a week away, I decided that I would try a run. The first shock was that my usual running gear wouldn't even fit, so in a cobbled-together ensemble, including the joggers that I wore during labour, off I set. It felt good to be outside in the fresh air, without a baby in my arms, just me, like it used to be. It's not that I didn't want to be with Ted, but everybody needs space and having just 15 minutes to yourself is enough to keep you sane. I got to the end of our street and felt fine. I'd heard horror stories about prolapses, but so far, all my bits were still inside my body and as far as I knew I hadn't wet myself. I got confident, turned my music up and enjoyed the dappled sun finding me through the trees in the park. The plan was to run through the park to the station, which is just less than a mile away, and back again. I know, I know, hardly more than a shuffle, but starting with a run that was achievable was better for me than aiming high and being hugely disappointed.

I made it home, breathless yet victorious. My body was my own again and I immediately felt less, well, wobbly. That could have been the beginning of a wonderful regime where I slowly got myself back in shape bit by bit, but the truth was that my feet didn't see trainers for another five months after that. Some people probably have stronger resolve, but for most of us, those few months after having the baby are a constant case of feeling on top of the world and capable one minute, and then low, vulnerable and really crap the next.

My only advice would be to maximise on the good days. Help permitting, try to get out to do something for yourself when you can. Something is always better than nothing. What helped me was just walking a lot with the pram. Every day during my maternity leave, I would set myself a goal of doing a walk of a certain length and reward myself halfway with a cuppa. Slowly, everything does shrink; in most cases the stretch marks fade a bit and the linea nigra, if you have one, gradually disappears. You look similar to the way you used to look. I say similar because it will never be the same. Your boobs are a bit softer, your nipples a bit more squishy. In my case, I have more cellulite, but in a good light, and from a certain angle, it's all OK.

BACK ON THE TELLY

I was back on telly just three and a half months after giving birth, and although I knew that some audience members would be cruel and judgemental of my appearance, I took comfort in the fact that most of our viewers are sensible adults who would be disconcerted and disappointed had I returned from maternity leave having lost an inconceivable amount of weight. I admit that it did bother me that I couldn't fit into any of my old clothes any more, and for at least the first six months back on screen I would be in a panic most days at 6pm, manically trying on dresses that were just a bit snug or shirts that were pulling across the bust. Everybody is, of course, different, but I've found that since pregnancy, my whole bone structure has changed; my hips are slightly wider, my back is broader. I'm a completely different shape and I had to start from scratch and learn what suited this new version of myself.

As we know, there is unnecessary pressure on mothers to 'get back into their jeans' and become impossibly slim just weeks after giving birth, fuelled mostly by unhelpful headlines about this so-called 'snap back' culture and unrealistic pictures of celebrities looking tiny in their first few weeks after having a baby. It's fair to say that some do snap back naturally and others manage it because they have the funds to pay for a nutritionist and a personal trainer, but those aren't the majority. For most of us, it takes a year and that is just the way it is.

It's a fact that it's unsafe to rush your post-partum recovery – and more importantly, how can you even think about dieting when you're breastfeeding and desperately need plenty of vitamins and nutrients in your diet to ensure that your milk is of the best quality, and you feel like you've got a permanent hangover without any of the fun and all you want is carbohydrates just to survive?

I did use one secret weapon though and that was a corset that I'd ordered from the States following the advice of my friend Tess. It's a simple compression corset that's approved for post-natal healing and I have to say that it was the best £50 I spent. It held me together, literally, and in the first few months, made clothes hang slightly better than they would have done otherwise. It's not a miracle cure, but wearing it every day helped somewhat with repairing my stomach muscles and pulling everything back to where it should be.

LOOKING AFTER YOURSELF

Everybody's birth story is different, but ultimately a woman's body, having completed the colossal task of bringing life into the world by means of a lengthy labour or C-section – which, let's not forget, is a complicated operation – usually feels depleted of energy, weak and exhausted. Yet, in the aftermath, all the focus is transferred to the baby without as much as a second thought for the mother, who, just hours after the birth, is putting in 24-hour shifts and getting to grips with feeding. Considering that with flu we'd usually be bed-bound for at least two days, that we don't have the time to recuperate after birth is extraordinary and baffling, but post-birth we also develop a new super power, and that's called being a mother.

As brilliant and brave as we all are, it's paramount that we look after ourselves post-partum, but good advice is often hard to come by. So, how should we be looking after ourselves in those first few weeks, what food should we be eating, are there any vitamins that could help? When is it safe to exercise and what exercises should we be doing? Well here's my friend, mother of three and personal trainer, Amelie, with some suggestions:

AMELIE
Life coach and trainer

I often get asked about fitness after a baby and what to eat to 'bounce back' quickly. My first answer is to take time to reacquaint yourself with your new body, to understand the changes it went through and to be its friend. My second answer involves a word that every new mum is now familiar with: perineum. It is the main area to come under pressure with pregnancy. And I mean physical, heavy pressure. It's also the area that may require cutting (episiotomy) during the delivery and therefore will be stitched. It's not as bad as it sounds, but as I discovered after my first pregnancy, it is vital to let it recover before you even start considering any form of exercise. I gave birth vaginally both times and had an episiotomy the first time around. I remember being three days post-partum and deciding to go for a walk with baby in the pushchair and husband in tow. I made it as far as the corner of my street before I needed to sit down. I had the feeling like *everything* down there was going to fall out. I couldn't believe that was happening to me, the 'fit' one!

When the midwife came for her weekly visit, I landed on her like a tonne of bricks detailing what had happened, and informed her that I was clearly a victim of medical error. I may even have threatened to sue. She looked at me, clearly trying not to laugh, and patiently explained that before I could do any form of exercise (long walks included) I needed to give my perineum time to heal and regain strength. This applies even if the delivery was via a C-section.

Once you've got your doctor's go-ahead (*do not start without it*), which is usually between four and six weeks post-partum, try to incorporate 20–30 minutes of exercise every other day. That can be divided into two bursts of 10–15 minutes each day. A mixed routine of heart-raising movements and strength-training is ideal. Think planks, mountain climbers, jumping jacks, tricep dips, split squats, walking lunges and toe reaches, which are all fairly low impact and make for a safe and effective workout. Bear in mind that the pregnancy hormone relaxin, which helped loosen up your ligaments throughout the last nine months, is still active for at least six weeks post-partum.

For those who don't have the time, energy or inclination to start a new fitness regime, I recommend ditching the car or bus and walking where possible. Taking long walks with the pushchair is another good way to shed the pounds and regain muscle strength. It also has the benefit of engaging your arm muscles and your core.

From a nutrition perspective, eating healthy, nourishing and satisfying food is the first step towards shedding the baby weight. Remember that it took nine months to gain the weight and it's not unusual to take between nine and 12 months to lose it. Sleep deprivation that comes with having a baby tends to slow the weight-loss process as cortisol levels are persistently high. This is the hormone that makes you reach for the cookie jar and a big portion of French fries. While it's perfectly fine to indulge, a balanced diet will fill you with the energy you need to keep going and feel good. The first step is to make sure your fridge and pantry are filled with white meat, eggs, wholegrain rice, pasta and bread, vegetables, fruit, nuts and yoghurt. Drinking at least 1.5 litres of water a day is a must, especially if you are breastfeeding.

In summary, having a baby plays havoc with our body, our hormones and our brain. It is the most natural thing to happen to us but it doesn't make it easy or simple. Time is your ally and listening to your body (and your mind) is hands down the best thing you can do before undertaking operation 'Pre-Baby Body Back'.

Be kind to yourself and good luck!

'I'd always wanted to breastfeed my baby when it was born and I recall very clearly a conversation with my sister about how it must be possible for everyone to do as otherwise how do babies in underdeveloped countries survive? That was before our daughter was born with a cleft palate, undiagnosed until day two and a day and night of the two of us trying to get her to take milk from me. It was a biological impossibility for her to feed from me, she couldn't suck. So after diagnosis I was handed a double electric breast pump.... and so our milking journey started for five months.' Pippa

MILKING IT

Feeding, as we know, is a controversial topic, maybe the most controversial when it comes to having a baby. At the very first appointment I had with my midwife at ten weeks, she asked whether or not I was going to breastfeed. It was a simple answer for me. Yes, I was. Most of us are pretty well versed in the benefits:

- It provides natural antibodies that help the baby resist illnesses.
- It lowers the risk of your baby developing asthma and other allergies.
- It helps their little digestive system to function better.
- It helps the mother to shrink the uterus back to its original size.
- It can help lower the risk of ovarian and breast cancer.
- It's free!

It's an absolute no brainer – well, at least it would be if only it was that easy. For some women, it's not even possible.

I honestly never considered that breastfeeding would be anything but a breeze and the midwife said nothing to make me think otherwise; she just nodded her head approvingly.

As I entered the third trimester we happened to have a 'breastfeeding expert' on our show. I'll mention no names but she is considered the number one in boob troubleshooting, and love her or loathe her, she is probably the most well-known expert in her field. During the rehearsal of the show she was also keen to know what my plan was in terms of feeding. I found her line of questioning incredibly intrusive, especially as we were all hooked up to mics, and the 30-plus crew and production team who were working on the show that evening could hear the entire conversation, which was largely about my boobs.

The more I tried to shut down the conversation, the more vocal she became about why I definitely 'must' breastfeed. I hadn't even disagreed with her. I wanted to feed Ted and I would try my best to do so, but I just didn't want to discuss it at that moment, on the studio floor. I could feel poor Matt Baker shifting uncomfortably at the mere mention of breasts. She left her book, which I must admit I didn't read. She was pushy, it wasn't helpful and I felt harassed by her line of questioning.

BREASTFEEDING — NOT QUITE A MASTERCLASS

'What's the first thing you think about when you hear the word "breastfeeding"?' asked our breastfeeding tutor. We all sat in a circle and she went around the group, one at a time. The men, all in their thirties at least, giggled like schoolboys. When it was Charlie's turn to offer something, he said 'Pain?' in a questioning tone. It turned out that he had hit the nail square on the head. That bitterly cold night in December, he became Mystic Meg and correctly predicted what my experience of breastfeeding would be, at least in the early days.

Each couple was handed a doll so that we could practise positions. I felt absurd as I held Baby Annabel up to my breast.

As we practised, there were more instructions from our tutor. 'Shout out some of the problems that you think may crop up when you're breastfeeding.'

We all looked blank. Problems?

A minute ago, the very same woman had told us how during skin-to-skin contact after the birth, the baby would snuffle about on our chest before 'finding' the nipple and beginning to feed. Just. Like. That. 'It's the most natural thing in the world,' she said. It will be 'magical' she said.

'Problems?'

'Just in some rare cases,' she quickly added.

We began racking our brains for past conversations with friends who were already mothers, but let's face it, until you're in it, it's just not that interesting.

'Mastitis?' offered Marissa with a questioning look.

'Good, yes. Anything else?'

Silence. We were out of ideas. The truth is that we all assumed that breastfeeding would just happen, that it would be, as our tutor had told us, 'natural, easy even'. We were then handed cards with potential 'problems' on them. She read out each card: thrush, latching problems, engorgement; gave a few solutions to each scenario and swiftly moved on. We covered it all in ten minutes.

We moved on to an old V.H.S. We watched a New Zealand breastfeeding expert manhandling a new mother who was having difficulty feeding. We were so distracted by her unnaturally deep voice and huge hands that made the patient's breasts look teeny weeny when she grabbed them that we couldn't concentrate. To be fair, we were more concerned with the tea and biscuits, which were being handed out at the same time. Back in our coats in the foyer, two hours after we arrived, we all agreed that we felt as unprepared for breastfeeding as we had before we set foot in the class.

THE TRUTH ABOUT BREASTFEEDING

Here's the truth. Breastfeeding is bloody hard. Each person's experience will vary, naturally, but show me a mother who absolutely nailed it 30 minutes after giving birth and continued to nail it for the first three months of the child's life. There's always a problem. Either the baby won't latch easily, which results in a plethora of nipple problems, or the baby will latch but loves the boob so much that they then won't take a bottle. I'd love to include a story here from a woman who experienced her little baby 'finding' her nipple, latching on perfectly and drinking her dry and then moving seamlessly to a bottle, but I didn't get one. These women must be out there, but one thing is absolutely for sure: they are NOT the majority.

Why aren't we told how difficult it can be from the off? I appreciate that the breastfeeding mafia out there will say that it's because they don't want to put women off, but in most cases, mothers will *always* do the very best they can for their child and will try to breastfeed unless they feel strongly against it. The majority will have weighed up the options and will choose what they believe is the best for their baby. What we absolutely don't need is women banging on about how breastfeeding is absolutely the only option without giving solid facts about how difficult it can be. The constant peer pressure and presumption is intimidating, even for an older mother who usually listens to her own instincts!

I strongly feel that being armed with the facts and knowing that feeding can be, and often is, problematic would have helped me prepare mentally for the tough road ahead. It would also have been a comfort to know that many women are in the same position. This lack of honesty leads to women feeling like failures for not feeding, and frankly, that is the last thing you need at 3am when you're awake trying to get your baby to latch while your partner snores. It's a lonely place to be.

> 'My partner works nights so I thought that the best decision was to bottle feed so that the nights when he was home he could take over the night feeds and I could sleep. It never crossed my mind to breastfeed. On the second evening I became poorly with an infection. I couldn't look after my baby so the midwives took him for a while so I could rest. He could be fed by them because I had chosen to bottle feed. Night times it was me and baby. I made sure that I had plenty of skin to skin contact with my little boy. Lay in bed with him and tried for that bond that I thought I should have with him. Of course I loved him, but it crossed my mind that if I had breastfed would we have been closer? My son was very irritable at times. I sometimes thought that was because it was me. He didn't like me. Over the coming weeks it became apparent that the colicky baby that we had also had silent reflux and a dairy allergy. All the time I was thinking breastfed is best. My experience has taught me that although I was adamant that I wanted to bottle feed and that I wanted to share the responsibilities with my husband and family, the reality is that when my baby arrived I had completely different feelings.' Charlotte

LATCHING ON...

Due to complications after the birth, I couldn't feed Ted until three hours after he was born. I was aware of the importance of colostrum and how you absolutely need to get that into your baby, even if you don't continue to feed, and so I became increasingly anxious, aware that my brand-new baby needed some nutrition and pronto. At the first opportunity, with two very inexperienced midwives overseeing proceedings, I carefully placed Teddy on my chest, waiting for the magic. Nothing happened. He didn't even move. We looked at each other and back at Ted. Why wasn't he rooting and finding the nipple? The midwives looked on, their brows furrowed, looking at me and then at their watches, stressing the point that time was marching on and that this baby needed to feed. Shattered from birthing, feeling exposed and hopeless, I shifted Ted closer to the source. Nothing was happening. Charlie tried to drown out the sighs of the midwives with gentle encouraging tones. 'Don't worry, Al. He'll do it now.' We all waited, eyes trained on this new little baby who was supposed to miraculously find my nipple and know exactly what to do with it. The midwife lost her patience and put one hand on the back of Teddy's head and the other firmly on my breast. She then stuffed my nipple unceremoniously into Ted's tiny mouth and held his head in position, him suffocating on a mouthful of boob.

The whole thing was barbaric, functional and devoid of any of the magic that we'd been promised. It was my mistake to let the midwives intervene; I should have been firmer. They themselves were young, inexperienced and, more importantly, had never been in the same position. I wish I knew then that this manhandling would lead to a world of pain and sore nipples that would blight most of my feeding experience. **So for any mothers-to-be: stay strong, mamas and DO NOT let anybody manhandle your boobs. Take your time to get it right, and if you end up needing a helping hand, urge them to be gentle.**

'I had no problem with my baby breastfeeding but then she wouldn't stop, ha ha! I gave up after 4 months because I was doing it exclusively and so tired. I'd taken the midwives advice not to give a bottle in the first few weeks at their word, even arguing with my Mum about it who totally disagreed. I ended up exclusive not by choice – my baby just loved it and would turn her nose up if a bottle came anywhere near her! No one could then feed her other than me which was tough – my partner or Mum couldn't share the load but all the while the midwives loved me and I ended up being a bit of a poster girl for going exclusive and for my baby taking to the breast so well. Meanwhile at home I was exhausted exclusively breastfeeding round the clock like that. Don't get me wrong, the bonding is lovely and I did feel very lucky that I didn't have any of the problems some of my friends did, cracked nipples or mastitis or any of that, but boy they don't tell you how tiring it can be going exclusive! I was so determined to do it all by the letter and perfectly, I ran out of energy by the end (the official guideline is to exclusively breastfeed for 6 months!).' Amy

Teddy did at least have some of Mother Nature's nectar, but that first clumsy feed led to a whole world of misery. The next six weeks would be the toughest of my life and for me is still the hardest part of motherhood to date.

173

By day two of breastfeeding I was already smothering my raw nipples in Lansinoh (buy some sort of lanolin cream *before* you give birth, so that you're armed and ready), so intense was the pain. I would dread feeding, and would swallow two Ibuprofen and two paracetamol before every feed. In those early days, it was worse during the night when it feels like they are cluster feeding, constantly attached to your breast. Like any pain, it feels worse when you're tired, and on little sleep, it felt like my raw nipples were being doused in vinegar every time he latched on.

The hellish early days

For the first few nights, seeing his little hands move in his crib, indicating that he was awake, would fill me with dread, like watching a piranha in a tank. Getting him to latch on through bleary eyes was really hard work. Luckily for me, Charlie was super supportive and would hold little Teddy's hands still as I squashed my breast into a burger shape so that he could take a good mouthful.

Three days after we brought him home from hospital, we noticed that Teddy had blood in his vomit when we winded him. Cue an apoplectic reaction from both Charlie and me. Shit, quick – call the NHS helpline. It was, of course, blood that he had swallowed from my nipple and was absolutely harmless as far as Ted was concerned, but it gives you a clear indication of what was going on in my bra.

The discomfort went up a gear when my milk came in. Just to complicate matters, my milk was delayed because I had lost so much blood post-birth. This is quite a common problem apparently, and does make feeding extra tricky, but not a single person at the hospital so much as mentioned it. It's also very common for women who have had a C-section.

'I was induced because of my age, but my daughter still didn't come for three days, and I had to have a C-section. Despite all the "too posh to push headlines", it is not an easy option – the recovery time is so hard, and when I was already struggling with breastfeeding (and putting a huge amount of pressure on myself to get it right, in part because I was older and I wasn't used to not getting things spot on), it was not the best start.' Vikki

However, when my milk hit, it hit hard. My breasts were on the brink of explosion. They were colossal, full to capacity and looking pretty awesome, according to Charlie. I thought that the timing of that particular observation was a bit off.

I stood in the shower trying to massage and hand express these footballs that were glued to my chest. Anything to take the edge off. They were so big, ugly big, and Ted simply could not get his mouth around my nipple. When he did eventually manage it, he then couldn't empty my breast completely and the spare milk that was left would crystallise to create this stinging, hot sensation.

The single thing that offered any kind of relief was cabbage leaves in my bra! A new low. The crystallisation ultimately led to thrush, so, it was back to the Queen Charlotte hospital to see the lactation consultant, who prescribed antibiotics for Teddy and me. By this point, one breast was completely out of action as it was simply too painful and felt on fire, even to the touch.

This meant that I would feed on one and express with the other. As soon as one feeding session ended, I would then start on the milking process and the soundtrack to that is a noise that will never leave you. It is the closest thing to morphing into Daisy the cow. When you feel at your most unsexy, this is the final nail in the coffin.

Teddy lost the typical ten per cent of his birth weight in the first week, but due to unsuccessful latching he was struggling to put the weight back on. Midwife, then health visitor and finally a breastfeeding expert, came to the house and would patiently show me various positions and suggest nipple shields and a load of other gizmos that are supposed to help make feeding more bearable, but to no avail. The baffled consultant eventually realised that Teddy had tongue tie, which meant that he couldn't open his mouth widely enough to accommodate the breast and would end up chewing on the nipple, causing further damage. He was treated immediately with a straightforward snip, though it didn't really go very far to solving the problem.

> 'Breastfeeding just never seemed the best option for me, I wanted to be the best mummy I could possibly be and after looking at as much information regarding breastfeeding as possible and discussing it with my midwife I knew that formula feeding was the best option for me. After giving birth I remember looking over at my husband who was cradling our baby with such love and adoration and suggesting that Dad do the first feed. It was a beautiful moment and one I will never forget or regret. And we formula fed from then on. I now have two beautiful healthy, happy boys, and they were both formula fed. I have never regretted my decision, it was the best decision for myself, my baby and my family.' Helen

I continued to persevere, often feeding with tears cascading down my cheeks because I was in such excruciating pain. It got so bad by week three that I was having to cancel visitors, as the thought of trying to breastfeed while holding a conversation was impossible. Each feed would be a gritted-teeth experience. Even feeding in front of my family became impossible. They all knew how painful I found it, and my mum, dad and sister would sit there pretending to be engrossed in whatever was on the telly, but I could sense them wincing silently with me as Ted latched on. I'd get hot, sweaty and self-conscious before making my excuses and disappearing upstairs. On one rainy Saturday afternoon, I sat on my own in my bedroom for four hours solid trying to feed. I felt lonely and seriously pissed off with Mother Nature that I was the only one who could feed Ted. It's such a colossal disappointment when it's not going to plan. In hindsight, that phase was very fleeting, but at the time it was difficult to see the light at the end of the tunnel.

BREASTFEEDING
Clemmie Hooper, midwife

Breastfeeding has many benefits to both you and your baby and is a lovely way to share a very intimate, special bond. But sometimes the most natural of things are the most difficult and even with all the classes and books you read during your pregnancy breastfeeding can still be a real struggle. Ask for help and support from those around you. Neither your nor your baby have done this before and it takes time and practice to get it right. Try to get your partner to do all the other jobs so you can focus entirely on feeding your baby. And remember that the important thing is that your baby is fed safely, whether you choose to exclusively breastfeed, mix feed or formula feed; there is no one-size-fits-all solution – it's an individual choice and everyone is different.

My disastrous experience of feeding nearly led to postnatal depression. I knew that I was on the cusp, and I strongly believe that the only thing that saved me was the unwavering support of my family. Breastfeeding really is a team sport, and requires everybody in the house to be on board, particularly in the early days. The mother is the star player of course, but it's hard to make it work without a supportive team. By that, I mean that sometimes, especially in the first few weeks, you may be glued to the same spot for an hour at a time and so you will need willing volunteers to bring you the odd snack, glass of water (because you do get ridiculously thirsty) and to pass you the remote control or your mobile so that you can distract yourself. It sounds insane, but when getting your baby to latch is proving difficult, the last thing you want to do is unlatch in order to get the remote, yet one hour plus is a long time to sit in a room, thirsty and staring at a wall.

By the end of the first three weeks I was a broken woman, worried that my child wasn't gaining any weight and struggling with the pain. By this point even my midwife, who had strongly discouraged it at the beginning, was suggesting substituting breast milk with formula. Mum was also all for it as she watched me scream in agony. I blindly battled on in my usual 'head down and get on with it' kind of way and now, I honestly wonder why I did it. I mean, nobody gets a medal saying 'whoooooo, I breastfed my child' and more importantly, research suggests that formula-fed babies can thrive just as well as breast-fed babies. My bigger concern should have been that I was compromising my mental health and the happy mother, happy baby ethos should have been my goal, not doing what I felt pressured to do. Feeding then pumping on repeat was tedious and spirit-breaking, especially when on one occasion, I knocked over a bottle of breast milk that I had just pumped and had nothing in reserve to feed my baby.

That was the final nail in the coffin. Charlie silently grabbed the car keys and left the house, returning 15 minutes later with two small bottles of Aptamil. I bawled uncontrollably, accusing him of thinking that I wasn't capable, yet it was the best and kindest thing he could have done, because knowing that we had something in reserve to feed Ted should it all go completely pear-shaped helped me relax and from that point forward, things gradually got better.

There was a sudden change at around the six-week mark. From nowhere, Teddy latched on and it didn't hurt any more. An imaginary Hallelujah chorus erupted. The struggle had been worth it, because from that point on, I looked forward

Breastfeeding: the painful early days!

to feeding and then never wanted to stop. The intense love I felt for him in those moments when I would look down and see him feeding contentedly, his little eyes closed, knowing that he was relying on me to literally keep him alive, was incredibly powerful.

Boobs out in public

My plan was to stop in time for my fortieth birthday. It would mean that I would have fed for exactly eight weeks, and Charlie and I could stay away overnight, but when the time came, I just wasn't ready to stop. In fact, I couldn't bear the thought of it, and so I kept going until my return to work firmly put the brakes on it.

I have to admit that I enjoyed it a lot more when I was alone. I'm definitely not one of those women who are not comfortable with others feeding in public. You are literally keeping your baby alive, for goodness' sake, and should therefore be allowed to do it whenever and wherever you need to. I'm just not one of those mothers who are slick with a muslin. You see some who can casually drape a cloth over the shoulders and feed their baby while eating lunch and having a conversation. That sadly isn't me. I tried it, of course, because otherwise you would spend most of your day in the house. I mean, doesn't the three hours between feeds simply whizz by? The most disastrous occasion was in a local Pain Quotidien when I'd met up with some non-mummy friends. It was all going really well; they kept commenting on how relaxed I looked. I didn't feel it, but was happy that at least we had got to the cafe without much drama, and Ted had been quiet so far. Midway through a latte, Ted let it be known that he was thirsty, so without a second thought, I hoisted him out of the pram and went about hastily trying to undo my shirt and maternity bra, while trying not to drop him. I know, I know, leave the baby in the pram until you're all set, but it was early days and I still had that anxiety when Ted started crying in a public place. Ridiculous I know, but I would try to get my nipple into his mouth as soon as possible to muffle his cries. With Ted latched on, I then quickly threw a muslin over my shoulder, hiding my exposed breast, or so I thought… I was pretending to listen to the conversation around the table, nodding at intervals, but really all I was concentrating on was Ted. He kept falling off the breast, maybe distracted by the different surroundings. My latte went cold as I tried without any poise or elegance to get him back on my boob. My friend offered to take him to give me a breather and I accepted gratefully. Suddenly the conversation stopped and the table fell silent. My three friends were all looking at me. To my right, two waitresses who were taking orders at separate tables stopped to look over. I looked beyond them to the chefs in the open-plan kitchen, who were pointing and laughing. I looked down to find the muslin that had been protecting my dignity had fallen to the floor and that both flaps on the bra were unhooked, meaning that I was sat there, with both breasts swinging free while I appeared to be engrossed in a conversation. I know that the café is well versed in catering for mothers who are feeding and is very welcoming, but a woman sitting there with both boobs out without a baby even near was edgy even for them. Red-faced,

I quickly covered my modesty, made my excuses and left with a now screaming baby. I hurried home, confidence shattered.

I tried to continue feeding when I went back to work, but it wasn't to be. I tried pumping between our afternoon meeting and our rehearsal and then between rehearsal and the live show but there was never enough time and your body seems to know when you're up against it timewise and rarely plays ball. After three weeks back at work, my supply was waning and despite scary amounts of **fennel tea** and **milk thistle**, which are meant to help boost your supply, plus pumping for hours after finally arriving home at 8.30pm, nothing was helping, and it was soul-destroying. I have so much respect for women who make it work, but I just couldn't. It made me so sad, and although I continued for a long time to do the first feed of the morning and the last feed at night, eventually I knew that Teddy was getting hardly any milk. One morning Charlie quietly prepared a bottle of formula and fed Ted. That was it, breastfeeding was over. I'm glad that in the end it just happened organically. I think had I built it up as the last feed I would have potentially drowned poor Ted in sentimental tears.

Switching to formula was a revelation. It lightened the load in so many ways. That was the turning point when I finally started to feel like myself again and even the baby weight finally started to disappear. I know they say that feeding shrinks the uterus, but breastfeeding also ensures that the body holds on to fat stores and in my case my body had a vice-like grip on those stores until breastfeeding was done. Giving Ted a bottle of formula and knowing how much he was drinking meant that on a good night we were sleeping through from

11pm to 7am, and more importantly that Charlie could feed him, which really helped cement their bond.

Feeding was my biggest battle in the early days of motherhood, but I'm glad that I persevered. I would try it again, but next time, I'd be armed with a bottle of formula from the very beginning and I wouldn't be scared to use it if times got tough. I'd also switch to combination feeding a lot sooner, but that's just me. The key is to ignore all others and do what YOU think is right for you and your baby. We're all grown-ups, for goodness' sake. Do what you want.

'I type this as I proudly watch my beautiful eight month and 16 day old (adopted) daughter roll around her playmat while happily babbling away to herself. My daughter was relinquished at birth. It was a decision her brave birth mum had taken during pregnancy. At the point of birth they were separated immediately so there has never been any contact between my daughter and her birth mum. My daughter was moved to foster care the next day. As such, formula was the only option. My daughter came to my husband and me at nine weeks and five days old. She was and still is a healthy, lively and smiley little girl who exceeds all her milestones. She has no health concerns whatsoever (apart from her current snotty nose!) We had three weeks to prepare for her arrival. We knew nothing of caring for a baby. We found ourselves looking for prams and nursery furniture, which is something I was resigned to never having to do. Bottles and nappies were terrifying but we've done well! She has always had a good appetite and is now weaning with gusto. I do not feel formula has held my daughter back in any way. I avoided some mother and baby classes to avoid the talk about boobs but other than that I don't feel judged. I get my baby's bottle out with pride!' Siobhan

MY TOP TIPS
(if you decide to breastfeed)

1

Always ensure that you have everything that you might need around you for the next 45 minutes before you start feeding.

2

Always have a bottle of water by your bed for those thirsty night feeds.

3

Wear a hair bobble on your wrist and switch it over every time you feed to remind yourself which breast you fed from last. Believe me, in the fog of the early days, this will be a godsend. There are also some great apps out there to help with this; Baby Connect is a good place to start.

4

If breastfeeding is proving difficult, ask the nurse at the hospital to check whether your baby has tongue tie. Early detection will prevent some heartache later on.

5

If you're using powdered formula, boil the kettle first thing in the morning and fill all five bottles that you'll need for the day so that you're not having to wait for water to cool when your baby has decided that he or she needs food NOW and is screaming the place down. All you have to do then is add formula.

SLEEP OR LACK OF IT

'Ah congratulations, both... you do know that you're never ever going to sleep again.'

That was the bog-standard greeting from nearly every parent when I was pregnant with Teddy. Some parents just love dishing out advice and the worst culprits are those who can barely remember the baby years and enjoy spreading fear in a smug 'I've been there, done that and got the bags to prove it' kind of tone.

The good news is that it's all bollocks and you *will* sleep again, just never as deeply or soundly and never for eight hours at a time, not even when you finally have a long-awaited night away without your child, because your body clock helpfully resets itself once you have a baby and you quickly realise why your own parents have a weird habit of always being up at 7.30am, even at the weekend, regardless of whether they're looking after the grandchildren or not. It's a by-product of having children.

I've looked at many surveys hoping to get a definitive answer about how much sleep new parents actually get. Unsurprisingly, they all vary, but on average, it is thought that mothers of newborn babies have less than three hours of unbroken sleep per night. It's less than that right at the beginning because your baby needs to be fed every two and a half hours. Another article suggested that parents to newborns miss out on SIX MONTHS' WORTH of sleep in the first two years of their child's life, sleeping on average 5.1 hours per night. I know, I know, seeing it down in black and white makes it all look so daunting, but like everything, there will be good times, bad times and life-zapping horrendous times.

Every single night is like playing Russian roulette. Even now, when Teddy is nearly ten months, we creep upstairs, *Matrix*-style, avoiding all the floorboards we marked out early on as perilous; we both go about our ablutions silently, running the tap for milliseconds for teeth brushing and definitely not flushing the toilet, then, when we have both finally got to our bedroom at the other end of the landing, we have the same futile conversation in a loudish whisper: 'Do you think he'll sleep tonight?'

'Don't know, I'm worried that he might be too cold.'

'Shall I check on him one more time?'

'No!!! You'll definitely wake him.'

'Do you have the monitor?'

'No, I thought you had it?!'

'Shit!'

'Well go back down and get it.'

'You go, you're lighter on your feet.'

I refuse, Charlie ends up going and Teddy is sometimes already awake by the time he gets back upstairs. In our first year of parenthood, that nightly jeopardy and not knowing how things may pan out between 11pm and 7am has proven to be the number one toughest element of being parents to a young baby.

The sleep thing never goes away. The other niggles seem to

dissipate eventually, but sleep seems to happen in cycles unless you've been particularly unlucky. In most cases, you'll have a few good nights, even good weeks and think you've nailed it, and then after one particularly horrendous night, the pattern will be broken and you'll unceremoniously be back to square one. You will spend hours guessing why this is, and how this could possibly have happened. Could it be: a. a fever? b. the four-month regression? c. a growth spurt? d. the clocks going forward? e. the clocks going back? f. a blocked nose? g. the dreaded teething? The list of possibilities is endless and until they can speak you will never, ever know for certain why your baby decided to be awake from 4.41am.

> 'Sleep...? What sleep?! It's not great, but it does get better – you have to remember, it does get better. You will survive!' Wendy

NEWBORN

It starts the minute you arrive home from the hospital.

I remember our first night vividly. This one single night is the biggest wake-up call of all. After a feast prepared by Mum of steak pie and veg as she tried to 'feed me up' and increase my iron, we, as a new family of three, went up to bed for the first time. My sister's advice was to go to bed as late as possible in those early weeks so that at least the inevitable long and lonely night in front of you is as short as it can be. It turned out that that was a great piece of advice. Every night for the first three or four weeks we waited until 1am, sometimes even 2am, before we took Ted up to bed. I would leave the last feed as late as possible in the hope that we could put him down straight after that, and on a good night, I'd have two hours of unbroken sleep before waking up for the next onslaught, which felt like a luxury at the time.

The first time we put him into the crib, he looked teeny, tiny. It was much like putting a squirrel to bed in terms of size. Then we stood and watched, completely silent, listening to his erratic breathing (which, thankfully, after a quick google we found was normal). He would snuffle like a hedgehog, unable to settle, all at sea and feeling exposed after being in the warmth of my womb for ten months. Think about it though – which other mammals apart from humans sleep separately from their young? Have you ever seen a cat in one basket with her kittens in another? It's bonkers and so the baby's struggle is understandable.

The snuzpod is a brilliant invention and without doubt the safest compromise to co-sleeping, but Teddy, in the early days, hated it and would make the shrillest, most heart-breaking cry on contact. Perseverance paid off, though, and sometimes he would drift off for short bursts, but mostly I would cave in and fall asleep around 5am and he would end up sleeping on my chest. Cue the emails with 'bad mother' in the subject line. I know it's hugely controversial and the potentially tragic consequences are not to be taken lightly, but show me a parent who has never ever done it – not even once?! For a few weeks the snuzpod was just another storage surface for bottles of water and blankets. I adored the times that he would sleep on my chest and those times are still some of my most precious memories, but we knew that we needed to remedy the situation fast and find a safe solution.

Quickly we learnt that two things really helped him settle in the crib. The first, a hot water bottle wrapped in his swaddle cloth and placed on the mattress to warm it about 20 minutes or so before we went up; and another tip from my midwife that seemed to work was if I placed the T-shirt that I'd been wearing that day in the crib so that he had my smell nearby. Basic, but it did improve things significantly.

> 'One tip I got from a friend was to place lots of photos of my partner and me close to the crib; apparently it helps to soothe them as they can still see "you". I didn't believe it, but it genuinely helped!' Alex

The first couple of nights are fine and you survive on hardly any sleep at all, the adrenalin pumping through your veins making you thrive on the lack of shut-eye, but gradually it wears you down. By the end of the first fortnight you experience this awful realisation that this situation isn't going away any time soon and you genuinely worry about how you will sustain this torturous pace. I'm good, great even, on very little sleep, but I really struggled with the fact that I was no longer in control of how much I slept, my baby was. It all came to a head one morning that had begun at 4.15am. I sat, zapped of energy, on a bed that desperately needed changing, surrounded by various glasses full of dusty water, mugs with grey tea at the bottom, feeding Ted in my pants and maternity bra. I cried as he clumsily nursed. I couldn't even be bothered to charge my phone that lay dead on the bedside table or to reach for the remote control. I was exhausted. Pre-baby, I'd often made some grand statements about how A.B.S.O.L.U.T.E.L.Y. knackered I was over a glass of wine on a Friday night, but in hindsight, I didn't know the meaning of the word. This is tiredness like you've never experienced before.

Experts will say sleep when the baby naps. From experience, this is practically impossible unless you are OK with living in an absolute pigsty. When they nap, your instinct is to race downstairs and try to fill/empty the dishwasher, fill/ empty the washing machine, sterilise bottles, order some shopping online, hoover and plump cushions ready for visitors and, potentially, if there's any time left, brush your teeth, wash your face or comb your hair. You'll have to prioritise as it's doubtful you'll get to all three.

The way I dealt with it eventually was to simply accept that my sleep was going to be broken for the foreseeable future and there was nothing I could do about it. This was a revelation. Suddenly I stopped counting the hours and felt calmer about it, and significantly less tired. Acceptance is the first step to recovery and all that. The good news is that your body is clever and will help compensate for the lack of sleep. Dr Chris Idzikowski, director of the Edinburgh Sleep Centre, explains that when your body eventually gets the chance to drop off, it knows that the two hours of deep, restorative sleep is priority and so that will come first in your sleep cycle.

It's tempting, especially in the early days, for one of you, usually the dad, to avoid the madness and head for cover in the spare room so that at least one of you gets a good night's sleep, but remember that old saying: 'There is strength in numbers.' We decided early on that we would try to remain in the same bedroom, even though I was the one who ultimately had to wake to feed, and Charlie was working and needed some semblance of sleep. Granted, he's a pretty deep sleeper and although he didn't always stir when I was hauling Ted out of the crib for the fourth time in a night, just having him next to us was comforting. Being on your own with a screaming baby in the first couple of weeks can be overwhelming and lonely, so even a sleepy 'You OK?' from your partner can seriously cushion the blow.

Take comfort in the fact that it did get a lot easier after the first six weeks and Teddy would sometimes go from 12am through to 5am without a feed, meaning that I could have a decent bit of sleep. Apart from the odd explosive nappy – a sight you have never seen the like of before, which would mean both of us being up and in the worst-case scenario changing his crib sheets, our bed sheets and my pyjamas (yep, that happened a few times, we even have pictures to prove it) – we fell into a rhythm and good old Ted was pretty compliant.

Everything changed again the minute we decided to move Teddy into his nursery. The first night was, as I expected, a disaster. Initially, he fell asleep at 7.15 while taking his last feed and, having placed him gently in the cot, I skipped back downstairs thinking that we'd nailed it. You see, historically, well, as historically as things get when you're discussing a six-month-old, once Ted was down, he was down, and apart from a few trips to stick the dummy back in, he would more or less sleep solidly, well, apart from between weeks eight and 12, oh, and then there was the four-month regression... but hey, such is babies. So anyway, down I went, the red wine was poured and I was confident that the move was done and dusted. Seamless. We joked about all the books gathering dust on the shelf in the lounge, that guided you through this process step by step. Money for old rope, we thought. We raised our glasses. 'To having our room back.'

As soon as the glass had touched my lips we saw a light flicker on the monitor. One light became four as Teddy's movements increased in the cot upstairs and soon his wailing was reverberating through the kitchen. I went back and forth four or five times to pop his dummy back in and roll him back to a comfortable position in the cot, and not widthways with his little head pushed up against the bars. We were unperturbed; we reasoned that this was normal and he was just adjusting to a new bed, like we all would. We knew that him still having a dummy was going to make it tricky and in hindsight we definitely should have got rid of that before the move, but hey, we were where we were. Should you or shouldn't you use dummies is an age-old argument that I rarely see anybody agree on. We felt our way and by now Teddy can take it or leave it and doesn't need it to sleep, but it's everybody's own call to make.

At midnight, we made our way to bed. As I went to push open the nursery door to kiss him goodnight, Charlie grabbed my arm to stop me and said, 'Don't, Al, you'll just wake him.' He was right of course, but it took all my strength to walk past the door and carry on to our room without him in my arms. Suddenly I wasn't ready for this change. I got undressed, my eyes never moving from the empty snuzpod that occupied my side of the bed. It seemed like a monumental shift, our baby's first steps to becoming independent, and the separation felt unbearable.

I got into bed with the monitor squished against my ear on the pillow. Charlie reasoned that I should move the monitor to the bedside table, sensing that my paranoia levels were at an all-time high. I did as instructed, but moved it back to my pillow the moment Charlie went off to sleep, which was precisely two minutes after the lights went off. I lay awake, looking at the mattress where Ted had slept from the day we brought him back from the hospital. Pathetically, I grabbed the blanket that hung over the side and breathed in the scent of him. Where had the last six months gone? I knew that it was the right decision to move him to his own room, it was time, but it felt all sorts of wrong.

An hour passed and I definitely wasn't sound asleep and feeling the benefits of this new arrangement. What if the connection between the two parts of the monitor was faulty? What if Ted had turned over and was stuck and suffocating? What if he felt lonely? I couldn't bear it. I pushed the covers off and crept as quietly as I could down the landing towards the nursery. I pushed open the door gently and felt my way along the side of the cot, the blackout blinds making it impossible to see anything. As my eyes adjusted, I could see him fast asleep with his comforter partly covering his face. I moved it away and made my way back to bed, relieved that all was well.

I finally slept… For all of about six minutes. The shrill crying on the monitor next to my face woke me with a start and off I trotted, retracing my steps back to the nursery. I felt around for the dummy, then Ted's mouth, and reconnected the two. Silence. He was asleep again and back to bed I went. I repeated this three times during the hour that followed. Charlie patiently suggested that I should leave him and wait to assess whether it was a 'proper' cry. I couldn't, and back and forth we both went endlessly with every slight murmur until 4.42am when Charlie finally snapped and said, 'Right, that's it, enough is enough. We have to just leave him.' It wasn't Teddy's sobs, but mine that then filled the dark bedroom. Sniffling pathetically, I tried to put up an argument. 'But… he doesn't know where we are, he's scared, and it is the first night!'

Charlie caved. He put his arm around me and shushed me to sleep. It was blissful, yet fleeting, as the monitor woke me again at 5.50 and this time, desperately needing to sleep myself, I scooped Ted up and took him back to the familiar surroundings of our bedroom, where between us he slept soundly until just past 8am.

I know, I know, we had tackled the whole thing badly. We should never have gone in as much as we did, we should have let him cry for a bit to see whether he could settle himself and we, well, I, definitely shouldn't have brought him into our bed. At least I made those mistakes so hopefully you don't have to.

The next night it was worse! Teddy was now in tune with the fact that he would be sleeping on his own in the nursery and he wasn't having a bar of it. By 7.30pm that evening he was absolutely exhausted and yet was fighting any attempt I made to lay him in his cot. His lungs, along with everything else, were developing at a pace and so his cries were earth-shatteringly loud. I didn't hear Charlie shout up the stairs that he was home above Ted's sobs and my desperate rendition of 'The Bare Necessities' from *The Jungle Book*, which usually calmed him. Charlie came up to find me wide-eyed, juggling Ted on my hip manically while trying to sing louder than his cries. 'What the hell is going on here?'

'Take him,' was all I could say.

Charlie then tried unsuccessfully to get Ted into his cot. The tears were now streaming down Ted's face. Proper tears, and the minute you become a parent you know the difference that proper tears make. This circus went on past 10.30 and our salmon that I'd bought from Sainsbury's for supper earlier still sat patiently in its vacuum pack in the fridge.

Ted had never really cried in the night; he snuffled and moved about a bit but was always asleep again the minute his beloved dummy was back in his mouth. We had been incredibly lucky. However, now the gloves were well and truly off and without Mama being within touching distance he was going to make damn bloody sure that we could hear him.

At 2.41am I jumped out of bed and pelted it down towards Ted's room. His little fists were hammering on the mattress. He looked me square in the eye and screamed, trying desperately to convey how unacceptable this new set-up was. My top tip now, and the one thing I always try to avoid, is looking Ted in the eye in the middle of the night. Once you've made eye contact, it really is game over and you know that you're in for a hellish couple of hours. Before this realisation, I shushed him, rubbed his tummy, rubbed his hair, turned on the mobile above the cot, checked to see whether he was too hot or too cold, sang more *Jungle Book* hits, tried teething crystals on his gums, got Ewan the Sheep involved... everything I could possibly think of, but nothing was working; his screams got louder, his mouth too wide for a dummy. Cue the next mistake ... I picked him up. I caved. I held him close, whispered sweet nothings in his ear and sure enough, the crying eased and his eyelids started to get heavy. Rookie mistake.

Despite me placing him back in the cot as carefully as you would an unexploded bomb, he instantly knew he was back behind bars and so the screaming started all over again. Eventually a baby inevitably tires him or herself out, and falls asleep – this is not to be confused with solving the problem, it's very much a temporary respite. Exhausted and unable to keep my eyes open any longer, I just curled up in a ball, on the floor beside the cot where I could just reach through the bars to put the dummy back in if necessary. I was a sorry sight.

An hour later and Charlie had come to investigate, having woken up and realised that I was still missing in action. His tall frame towered over me as I slept in the foetal position on the floor. 'Al... what are you doing, babe?' There was a hint of incredulity in his voice.

'I don't know... it was just easier to manage.'

'Come to bed.'

Ted heard our stage whispers and started shifting.

'No, it's easier if I just stay here.'

'Well at least get into the *bed*.' I did as I was told, got off the floor and climbed into the double bed that's just on the other side of the cot in the nursery. **Warning. Sleep deprivation makes you irrational.**

The interesting thing about our generation is that it seems that we are having approximately half the amount of sleep that our mothers had. They, on average, would enjoy a luxurious six hours. What? How? I can hear you all scream in unison. Well, the answer is a pretty seismic culture shift in attitudes towards child-rearing and the rise of the baby monitor. More information means that our fear of SIDS is at an all-time high and us late starters are the main culprits when it comes to investing in high-tech baby monitors and mattresses fitted with alarms. It's completely understandable, of course, but it also results in us being more fretful and consequently more wakeful. When deciding on a monitor, we, after much debate, went for a halfway house and used an audio monitor as opposed to a video monitor as I would end up glued to it like *Big Brother*. You can't really win though because even if Ted does have a very good night's sleep, I end up fretting and shaking the monitor to make sure that it's working, then straining for any noise. I have frequently decided that it's too quiet, that we haven't seen the monitor flash, and so I end up running to his room shouting, 'Oh my God... I think he's stopped breathing!' Me? Overdramatic?

> 'A standout moment has to be the effect that sleep deprivation had on us; my husband had a recurring dream that our son was in the bed with us – we've never even co-slept!' Karina

The days of late nights are out of the question, although we often cave at the end of a long week and get overexcited that we can have a few glasses of wine, just the two of us, and remember what we were like before Teddy. You will cave too, but do it at your peril. The next morning feels hellish, but sometimes dancing in the kitchen till 3am, knowing full well that your baby will wake approximately three hours later, is most definitely worth it. Some time together can reset you and make the whole debacle a lot more doable even though you're more knackered.

During this first year, I've spent most of my time in a constant daze, with a slight headache, bloodshot eyes, sallow skin, a dry mouth and a penchant for carbs. It's like a constant hangover without any of the fun – apart from the odd late-night boogie in the kitchen. It raises the question of how on earth we're capable of looking after a child all day after a hellish night, but we do, we just get on with it, in the same way that parents have been doing for generations.

The glaringly obvious difference is that us lot have decided to have children later in life when, naturally, our energy levels should be depleted in comparison to twenty-something mums and dads. In all honesty, I think that we absolutely can keep up with the younger parents. I mean, most of us look after ourselves a lot better these days, thanks to the fact that we want to be active parents for as long as possible. I think the main cause of exhaustion in your mid-thirties to early forties, which is unavoidable after you return to work, is the beastly combination of a demanding job plus a demanding baby. It's brutal, but you'll grit your teeth and just about manage. At least us lot have had enough practice at being tenacious – a bit of sleep deprivation isn't going to take away the joy of having a baby... well, it might do some days, in fact, it might feel utterly joyless especially when teething starts, but, you know, bigger picture and all that.

You, like us, will probably have the daily who's more tired argument. 'I'm tired.'

'What? You didn't even hear him when he woke at three thirty.'

You know that one? We promised ourselves we wouldn't fall foul of it, but it happens every morning, most evenings and sometimes in the middle of the night on the landing.

Slowly, we have found our rhythm. Charlie puts him down in the evening, following a basic routine of bath, babygro, bottle, bed, which, let's face it, sometimes works and sometimes doesn't. He's patient and able to stand there listening to Ted's cries until he drifts off without caving in and picking him up. I'm hopeless at this as I find it virtually impossible to listen to a crying baby. I can't help it, it's just the way I'm programmed, and so in the middle of the night, it's usually me who runs to the nursery at the first flash of the monitor while Charlie snores away, oblivious. I'm better on less sleep and Charlie is more likely to lose his rag at night, so this is how it works for us.

There is no doubt that sleep deprivation and all the side effects that come with it is hard slog – I mean there's a reason why it's used as a torture method – but all parents will agree that it's insignificant in comparison to having your own child to love. It's par for the course and all too soon it will be a distant memory, gone in a blink of an eye. One day soon we'll long for those nights when we felt closest to our baby, remembering how their little babygroed body felt in our arms, their soft cheek against ours, as we cradled them tenderly, the only ones who could really comfort them.

I'll try to remember that tonight as I stand bent over that cot, eyes closed in frustration, wishing that this phase was over.

> 'Throughout the second pregnancy I just didn't think of my experience with Marnie as a newborn because the whole possibility that I could end up having another colicky, difficult baby scared the hell out of me! I used to think I have done it once I can do it again!!!But good job I didn't worry too much because Louis has been a complete dream.' Naomi

SARAH OCKWELL-SMITH
Sleep expert and bestselling author
of *The Gentle Sleep Book*

A baby's brain triples in size during the first twelve months of life – holding and comforting your baby when they cry plays a big role in this development, and is important to do at night as well as in the day. Use your instinct and pick your baby up when it feels right, and don't beat yourself up over 'caving in' – you have instincts for a reason!

'We read all the sleep books – literally all of the books. What really helped was starting a sleep diary for Harvey, to help us track any patters and uncover his habits. I've got friends who tried Controlled Crying, others who swore by a 'No Cry' approach – at the end of the day every baby is different, and not every routine works for everyone. That's where the diary was really helpful – I felt I had a much stronger grasp on how Harvey sleeps.' Aisha

'When Norah was first born we had every intention of putting her into a strict sleep routine. We were adamant we wouldn't fall into the trap of letting her in our bed. Fast forward three weeks and she was sleeping with us every night! It was a nightmare as you can imagine but we didn't know what else to do! She woke every hour or so for a feed and sometimes would be awake for over 3 hours at a time. (Just thinking about it now is horrible!!!) Thankfully a family member introduced us to their 'baby sleep bible' otherwise known as *The Sensational Baby Sleep Plan* by Alison Scott-Wright. Within three days of implementing the plan Norah was sleeping in her own room for 12 hours with no feeds and no visits from us at all! She also has three set naps a day. Regardless of her mood, whether she is awake or not even now she will happily go to bed or go down for her naps. The book is an absolute GOD SEND!! My partner and I finally have our lives back!! I can't recommend it highly enough, I tell absolutely everyone about it! We have gone from having an extremely cranky, clingy and upset baby to a totally contented one who is an absolute joy! All because she now gets enough sleep.' Jade

THE THREE MOST COMMON
SLEEP-TRAINING APPROACHES

1

Self-soothing: this approach helps your baby to settle themselves; generally you put your baby to bed when they are drowsy (so before they fall asleep on you!). The hope is that they then associate the bed with sleep, as opposed to you. Try not to pick them up right away, to help encourage them to soothe themselves.

2

Controlled crying: this is a rather more controversial method that involves not picking your baby up, but leaving them to cry for specific and timed periods – a more extreme version of self-soothing.

3

No cry: the method that allows you to have a more flexible approach to bedtimes, and to stay and comfort your child while they go to sleep.

Whatever route you take, it's important to be consistent – it's no use trying controlled crying for two days, only to switch to 'No cry'! Give your little one a chance to get used to it, and remember that what works will also be dependent on your baby's very individual personality. Most importantly, don't panic – you'll get there!

TINY BABY = HUGE ANXIETY

Even more angst-inducing than feeding and sleeping troubles is the weighty responsibility of keeping your little human alive in the early days. Even something as minor as a sniffle can throw you into a head spin.

I don't think I actually knew what proper worry or anxiety was before I became a mother. I mean, I thought I did. Like you, I've had many a sleepless night worrying about work, fretting over finances, concerned about completing endless to-do lists, but nothing compares to the intense anxiety that comes with being a mother. The potency of the love that you feel for your baby is equalled only by the strength of anxiety you feel when he or she is in pain or upset. There are a few occasions that I can recall when these feelings were really cranked up to the max, the first of which was Teddy's eight-week injections.

THE FIRST SET OF INJECTIONS

I dreaded those first injections from the day Teddy was born, and the night before, I lay awake, watching Ted sleeping soundly in his crib, imagining needles puncturing his tiny arms and legs. I'm not even scared of needles – I really don't mind a quick injection and take them in my stride – but the thought of such pain being inflicted on my little boy was too much to bear.

I recruited Mum for some moral support, which, as it turned out, was the best thing I did. It sounds pathetic coming from a grown woman but I'd highly recommend taking someone with you at least to the first session, which is by far the most torturous. With Ted sandwiched between us in his car seat, we sat silently in the waiting room at the surgery waiting to be called, the ticking of the clock on the wall counting us down to the dreaded deed.

'Edward Thomson,' came the shrill call of the nurse as she stuck her head around the door, eyes searching the waiting room.

'Yes.' My voice was small, nearly inaudible.

We stood in unison, scooped up Ted and walked as slowly as if we were heading to the gallows. First was a weigh-in with the health visitor, and, all too familiar with dealing with new and nervous mothers, she tried her best to make small talk, sometimes raising her voice to muffle the ear-bleeding cries of other babies in the nurse's room. I kept nodding and smiling, but her friendly demeanour did nothing to soothe me. We sat again and waited for the nurse, the cacophony of noise from her room foreboding.

It was our turn and I fumbled pathetically with the poppers on Teddy's sleepsuit, hands shaking, all fingers and thumbs. Mum took over. The nurse explained what injections Ted would be having that morning. The first was the 6-in-1 vaccine that would protect against diphtheria, hepatitis B, Hib, polio, tetanus and whooping cough. I appreciate how lucky we are in this country to have the NHS, who provide these expensive jabs that will protect our little ones from life-threatening disease, but at the same time, that sounded like a beast of an injection for such a tiny baby.

It didn't end there. In the same sitting would be the Rotavirus vaccine, Pneumococcal vaccine and, last but not least, the Men B vaccine. Three meaty injections, and an oral dose, in one tiny body. Official literature insists that babies barely react to these immunisations and, if they do, it's nothing more than a mild reaction, a slight temperature for up to 48 hours. On the flipside, there are also plenty of anti-vac websites with strong arguments against immunisations. It really is a controversial topic that can divide parents. The 'antis' talk extensively about the fact that there is aluminium in baby vaccines and provide some case studies where children have become severely ill after having the jabs. I read many with interest, but on the whole, the solid examples I found were rare, and most of these were emotive and sometimes hysterical without enough factual content.

It pays to research

Having done lots of research, my friend Jana insisted that the vaccinations for her twin girls be staggered as she worried about a reaction. Another couple of friends have chosen not to vaccinate at all. We are fortunate to live in a country where we can choose. Being a parent is all about making choices and this is one of the early ones that you must decide on. It's a good subject to research during maternity, especially because some vaccinations like vitamin K and BCG, which are available in areas that are considered at a high risk from tuberculosis, such as West London where Ted was born, are offered straight after birth and you need to be able to make an informed decision. I was ignorant and under-prepared so my instinct was to accept NHS recommendations, but I really should have been more clued up.

Back to Teddy's first jabs...

With Teddy stripped to his vest, it was time to get the show on the road. The nurse asked me to read every label to check that I was happy with the dosage being administered. The weight of responsibility lay heavy on my shoulders as I read and re-read the tiny typed labels. 'I think they're OK,' I offered. 'Good. If you just want to hold him down as still as you can,' came the matter-of-fact instruction from the nurse. I couldn't do it. My hands were sweaty with nerves and he was slipping from my grasp. Without discussion, Mum took over. I watched on, welling up as little Ted, so unaware of what was to come, smiled up at his grandmother, full of good faith, while the nurse flicked the injection efficiently, ridding it of air bubbles with a latex-covered finger.

As I fought the strongest urge to snatch Ted up and run out of the door, the first needle was inserted, breaking his soft, perfect skin. There was a millisecond of silence as Ted digested what had just happened and then, like a grenade exploding, the pain hit and the most piercing, shrill scream I'd ever heard erupted from him, filling the room. The onslaught continued. He looked at me piteously, tears filling his eyes, and I wept too. I was convinced that Teddy would hate me for the rest of his life. As soon as the last one was done, I picked him up and offered him my breast, hoping that it would provide comfort. In between body-shaking sobs, he sucked gratefully, and gradually the hysteria subsided on both our parts.

The aftermath

With mascara smeared across my cheeks, my nose red and swollen and my maternity bra still undone, I went to the pharmacy in search of baby Calpol. The advice from the nurse was to give a dose as soon as possible after the injections. Even this went against the grain. I wasn't comfortable with giving my eight-week-old even more drugs for his little system to cope with and so I decided to ride it out, hoping that we wouldn't need it. Teddy slept for most of the day, a heavy stupor as his body processed the alien chemicals in his bloodstream, then at four o'clock, bam, he was awake, hot, sweaty and hysterical. Nothing would calm him. I fed, I rocked, I bounced, I sang and did it over and over again until I caved and gave him some medicine. Having tasted nothing but breast milk up until this point, he spat most of it up, wailing uncontrollably.

By 7pm, I was close to meltdown. Charlie came home and immediately went in search of the thermometer. Ours is similar to a scanner in a supermarket, so we stood around the crib zapping Teddy's forehead each of us in turn to compare. It wasn't good; his temperature was rising, and in just under an hour we were at 39 degrees centigrade. I knew that a high temperature in a young baby could lead to convulsions. In fact, my nephew had suffered one at ten months, so my paranoia was at an all-time high. While I furiously scoured the internet, Charlie tapped his foot impatiently, waiting for his call to be answered by the NHS helpline, and Mum rubbed Teddy's red cheeks, shushing him. Stress levels were soaring and a bad night ensued.

Teddy's temperature showed no sign of dipping despite the cold flannels and Calpol. He had bad diarrhoea and the constant crying left him exhausted yet too out of sorts to sleep. It was a long, gruelling eight hours, and Charlie and I felt like we had experienced for the first time what being parents really was like.

Thankfully, and exactly as the helpful advisor from the NHS helpline had predicted, Teddy's temperature was back to normal by the next morning, but he was still cranky. Sleepily, I pushed him around the kitchen island 108 times while singing 'Row, Row, Row Your Boat' before he fell asleep. I know how many times it was because it was only the counting that kept me awake, but gradually he recovered and returned to being the content, happy-go-lucky Ted we knew.

The other injections

I'm glad to report that although equally angst-inducing, the 12-week and 16-week injections were less of an ordeal. The 12-week is just a repeat oral dose of the Rotavirus, which Teddy gulped down greedily, and one booster of the 6-in-1, which he barely reacted to. The 16-week injections (which I put off until Ted was 20 weeks, hoping that the extra time would make him more hardy) also passed without too much drama. Again, this set involved three jabs, the third 6-in-1 and the second Pneumococcal vaccine and the second dose of Men B, and with me this time holding his chubby thighs, he took it on the chin and was upset for a fraction of the time. Apart from an unsettled night, there was no temperature or any other tell-tale signs. It was all over. We could now breathe a sigh of relief until the next lot, just after his first birthday.

The saving grace with immunisations is that they happen according to a schedule. You know they're coming and you can prepare for them, but when the first fever or cold hits, usually just when you've started to hit your stride, it often leaves you feeling like you're back at the starting line.

THE FIRST VIRUS

At the four-month mark Teddy suddenly changed from being a really good sleeper to a very bad sleeper. Bam! It literally happened overnight. The change was immediate, brutal and bloody hard to deal with. We'd never said it out loud but up until this point, we had lived the sleeping dream. This was nothing to do with our technique or knowledge, it just happened and we couldn't believe how fortunate we were.

One night though, and for no particular reason, Teddy just kept waking... Every. Single. Hour. Smugness quickly gave way to frustration, anxiety and desperation. The four-month mark was tricky at best...

Three major things coincided to create the perfect storm. First and foremost, there was the much-documented 'four-month sleep regression', added to that we were experiencing the first hot spell of the year and on top of that, Teddy got his first proper virus.

'It started with a cough...'

It started with a cough. I was so naive and thought that my clever boy had heard someone coughing and was simply copying it. I clearly remember commenting on his cute 'fake cough', my so-called maternal instinct completely failing me. It was only when a sneeze ended in his face and my hair being covered in baby snot that I realised that we may have a bit of a cold on our hands. I was unperturbed. It was no big deal, just a common cold.

> 'I never feel guilty in admitting Marnie was the most difficult, nightmare newborn to four-month-old I have ever known, and she can still be a challenge today – it's her strong personality! From pretty much day one she had the worst colic known to man and sometimes the crying would continue to her next feed time, so I would have had zero sleep in between, and the awful pattern would just continue full circle again. Those days were bloody tough and I look back and feel proud I managed to somehow get through!' Naomi

One terrible night later and Teddy was breathing like Darth Vader. My instinct told me that I needed to take him straight to the GP, and the very helpful doctor confirmed that it was in fact croup and prescribed a dose of steroids. I then visited four pharmacies trying to track down the medication. This was not ideal when Teddy was in the car seat and like a dead weight to carry around.

In desperation, I drove to the Queen Charlotte hospital, where he was born, thinking that they were bound to have the much-sought-after drugs there. I ran down the corridors, frantically trying to seek out Lloyds Pharmacy. Time was ticking and I had just had a text to say that the taxi to take me to work was already parked outside my house. Shit! The hospital chemist did have the medication but unfortunately couldn't possibly dispense a prescription that had been prescribed by a GP and not at the hospital... ARGH!!!!!!! I was now sweating profusely.

Luckily, we had picked up our nanny Jess en route and she was keeping a close eye on Ted in the back seat. The car was parked in the short-term spaces directly outside the entrance, which gives you 20 minutes of grace. Having had zero luck at the pharmacy, I was now trying to persuade the stubborn receptionist at the emergency department to let me speak with one of the doctors, who could then re-prescribe the medicine at the hospital so that the pharmacy could dispense this liquid gold. The receptionist just stared at me while repeating, 'I'm sorry, madam, it is a very busy morning, you will need to bring the baby in and then I will do my best to get him seen in the next four hours.' Four HOURS?! There was nobody there; the place was literally empty, not one other person. I'm ashamed to say that my response was less than polite. I stood there, knuckles white as I gripped the desk tighter and tighter.

'Where is the baby?' she asked.

'In. The. Car,' I replied.

She looked at me, horrified. I realised my mistake and added hurriedly, 'With another grown-up.'

It was too late. She clearly thought I was lying and went to pick up the telephone... Now, whether she was planning on calling for help or social services, I don't know, but I turned on my heel and ran back to the car, feeling massively guilty for no reason at all as the parking warden slapped a parking ticket on my windscreen.

VIRUS NUMBER TWO

Virus number two decided to pay us a visit just as Teddy had started to sleep through the night in his own cot. He was seven months old and had suddenly developed a rash, just on his trunk to begin with. Without missing a beat, I flew down the stairs to look for a glass. In my mind, I had already arrived at meningitis. Breathlessly, I rolled the glass gently over the angry red spots, which faded when pressed and meant that no, it wasn't meningitis. My next diagnosis was heat rash. 'It's bound to be.' Charlie and I were standing over the changing table, brows furrowed, while Teddy looked back at us quizzically. We conceded that it was nothing too serious and left it until the next morning.

'Charlie, I think he's got chicken pox,' I called from the nursery as I was changing Ted. Charlie was at my side in a flash. It was worse now, and there were single spots on his arms, legs and back.

'Right. Let's get him to the GP.'

The doctor's expression and tone instantly conveyed that he saw many first-time parents who like us were susceptible to jumping to conclusions. He didn't think it was chicken pox, probably a bit of prickly heat, and kindly suggested that, in future, we may want to have a look at the **NHS's visual guide to baby rashes that's available online** and, to be fair, is brilliant.

We thought we were out of the woods but then Teddy started coughing and sneezing later that day, and putting a snot-filled Teddy to bed that evening was impossible. The only thing that would calm him, and still does to this day, was Nelson's homeopathic granules. I normally rub some onto his gums. It's magic. Catnip for babies. His temperature was creeping up, and in our desperation we gave him the dummy, which in hindsight was a big mistake, but even that provided no comfort as it made it impossible for Ted to breathe. He eyed us pleadingly from the cot, willing us to do something to take away his discomfort. It was just a common cold, nothing serious, yet it broke my heart to see him writhing in frustration, desperate for sleep but unable to breathe easily enough to drift off.

It was time to get the big guns out. The snot sucker. Parents-to-be out there will now be gagging at the thought, especially when I tell you that it works by you sucking out the snot from your baby's nose through a tube. I know. I had the same initial reaction as you're having right now, but it works, and – more than that – seeing the snot collect in the bottom of the straw is oddly satisfying, sort of like seeing the Dyson fill up when you're vacuuming. Combined with a saline solution, this gadget is a miracle worker. Don't worry, snot doesn't get anywhere near your mouth, but it certainly does the job. We went through the whole rigmarole, snot sucker, infant Calpol, Calpol plug-in (which is genius), baby Olbas oil and, eventually, Ted was calmer and less congested.

The display on the digital clock showed 4.02am, and as I sat on the floor, forehead on the bars of the cot, stroking Ted's cheek, I thought about other parents around the world who were also sitting up with their children. I thanked goodness that we were dealing with a straightforward virus. I touched wood and reminded myself to always be grateful for good health and to never take it for granted. It's in those small hours that I've often had the most clarity over the last year.

'At the time of writing my little girl Lola-Mae is 12 weeks old. I never thought that we would all get this far, myself, my partner David and Lola. I am 40, nearly 41, and have experienced two miscarriages. When I became pregnant with Lola we were ecstatic, we got through the 12-week scan and every day was a milestone... We were discharged the next day after giving birth, and although I was glad to be going home, there was something niggling at me. Lola had hardly fed and I was worried about her. The midwife arrived at around 10am the next day; she took one look at Lola and called an ambulance; her lips had turned blue and she feared that Lola was lacking in oxygen. We went to the A&E department of our local hospital and were taken straight through to resus, where they laid my little tiny not-even-one-day-old baby on the big hospital bed. I sobbed, I never knew such love until I looked at my precious baby and realised I could lose it all again.' Wendy

DR SARAH JARVIS, GP

I go with a rule of three: Don't panic; trust your instincts; if in any doubt – seek medical help. In terms of how to stay prepared at home, I recommend that every parent have the following in their first-aid kit:

1

A digital thermometer. There are two options I recommend, either an in-ear thermometer or a digital thermometer that can be put under your baby's armpit. I do not recommend temperature strips, which are put across the baby's forehead, as they aren't accurate enough, or old-fashioned mercury-filled thermometers.

2

Ibuprofen liquid for fevers and pain. You can use Ibuprofen from the age of three months, at the right dose for their age, and I tend to find parents find it more convenient than paracetamol as it lasts for longer.

3

Paracetamol liquid, which can be used from the age of two months – I recommend this for babies under three months; any baby with chicken pox (where you shouldn't use Ibuprofen) or as an add-on to Ibuprofen if your baby is still in pain.

4

A first-aid manual to go in the first-aid box – if you're baby is ill, it's very easy to panic and forget everything you've learnt.

5

Antiseptic wipes, cream or spray for cuts and grazes.

6

Plasters (with scissors to cut them to size).

7

Sterile gauze dressings for bigger cuts, with micropore tape to keep them in place.

8

Tweezers to remove small splinters.

9

Rehydration salts to help keep your baby's hydration levels up if they have diarrhoea and vomiting.

10

A teething gel.

WHEN 2 BECOME 1: YOU AND YOUR RELATIONSHIP

◀▶

'You've lost your naughtiness.'

'What?'

'You've forgotten how to have fun.'

I could feel my anger rising. I'd made the fatal mistake of asking Charlie how he thought our relationship had changed since we'd had Teddy.

I pushed him. 'So, do you think it's better or worse?'

'Hmmm?'

'Do you think it's better or worse?'

'What's better or worse?'

Angry Birds on his phone was taking precedence and it was pushing all the wrong buttons.

'Our relationship!'

After a pause, while he completed the next level and then, avoiding the question, 'It's not better or worse, you just don't really want to have fun any more.'

I was so totally crestfallen that I couldn't manage an appropriate answer, so, loaded with as much sarcasm as I could manage, I went with, 'No, cos I hate fun!'

He gave me my least favourite look – it's a mixture of patronising and exasperated – and went to hide in the toilet, taking his phone with him.

I sat, stewing, going over what I'd just heard. When was I supposed to be having 'fun' with a seven-month-old baby, a full-time job and a list of chores as long as my arm? I mean, what did he want me to do? Forget that Ted is napping in his cot and going to wake any minute now for a purée I haven't made, and that I need to get his cot sheets out of the washing machine and into the tumble dryer so that they're dry by the time he needs to go to bed because he's been sick on the spare set this afternoon, and that the dishwasher needs emptying, bottles need sterilising and there's absolutely nothing for us to eat when he's finally been bathed and put to bed so I also need to go to the supermarket, but, forget all of that, let's open the wine and put some music on and dance in the kitchen until 4am like we used to.

I could hear the familiar sound of rugby highlights seeping from under the toilet door. Charlie had already moved on from the conversation. I hadn't.

He wanted it all: a woman who's trying her best to be a good mother with zero previous experience, who's also trying to juggle all that motherhood throws at her while holding on to a high-profile job on a daily show, while running a household and taking responsibility for more than 85 per cent of the organisation of *everything*! (That was in the moment exaggeration to be fair.) Oh, but hang on, she's not that great, because in the process she's forgotten how to be 'fun'. I wanted to punch him.

I sat in the same spot long enough for anger to finally give way to introspection. He was still on the toilet.

So what if I had become less 'fun'? Doesn't everybody after having a baby? But, was I so stressed about being a good mother that I had forgotten how to relax and have a bit of a laugh? Had I become... boring?

The conversation hadn't gone as I was expecting it to. I honestly thought that his answers would echo how I felt. That yes, our relationship had changed since having Teddy, because we were now a lot closer, more solid, because we'd learnt how to compromise and that seeing each other in a parent role had made us love each other more.

I put the kettle on. He finally emerged from the toilet, put his arms around my waist and kissed the top of my head.

'Stop it,' I said half-heartedly.

He didn't.

'I know you've been sitting here stewing, Al, but I'm not always gonna give you the answer you want. You could just do with relaxing a bit. Now, stop worrying so much and give me a kiss.'

I waited a few seconds, just to prove a point, and then slowly turned to face him. The monitor flashed and then a shrill cry erupted.

I sighed. 'Shall I go?'

THE MATHS OF RELATIONSHIPS

Charlie and I have been together for six years. We got engaged after four years, married after five and had a baby after six.

There is no doubt that all of it, but especially a baby, has put a different spin on things, to put it mildly. We used to be tempestuous, volatile and unpredictable. Now we are loving, unbreakable and predictable. I prefer this version of us, although having calmed down substantially since the conversation above, I can see what Charlie meant about the lack of 'fun'. I'm really hoping that time will help us rediscover that part of us. We're still adjusting.

A baby won't fix a problematic relationship. That's what people say, isn't it? The truth is that it'll do anything but fix it. You have to be made of pretty solid stuff before you can even consider raising a child. It will test you to the nth degree. It has made us fall both in and out of love with each other and has pushed us, sometimes grudgingly, to re-learn how to love each other now that we are a family.

Jumping from a twosome to a family of three is trickier than I expected. Before we had Teddy, Charlie and I, although we loved each other's company, would do quite a bit of socialising separately. We were independent, and respected the fact that we had separate interests and enjoyed seeing our friends on our own sometimes. When you have a baby, suddenly, you are together a lot more. Interests and friends naturally take a back seat and so you end up doing things as a family, but family time isn't the same as couple time. You are often together, but never alone.

It's not that we don't have a choice – Teddy's grandparents would love to baby-sit regularly while Charlie and I go off and have some 'us' time, but we just don't want to. While we crave time together, we both agree that being with Teddy is the priority, and because we work all week, weekends as a family are precious. The flipside is that finding time to have a conversation where we just focus on each other is tough, impossible some weeks, but we keep trying or else it all falls apart.

When I found out that I was pregnant, we were elated and the news had an instant effect on our relationship. Charlie became more protective and gentler and those first few weeks, as we got to grips with the fact that we were going to be parents, were up there with the best of times. We were excited, relieved and grateful that we had fallen pregnant without a hitch and were ready to swap our frenetic existence for family life. I suppose that's the joy of becoming a parent a bit later on – there's no fear of missing out, you've done it all and you're ready to embrace an equally hectic, but new, way of living. Those tender weeks were like being back in the early days of our relationship; we texted constantly like teens, with little emojis of babies or milk bottles, enjoying our secret.

Pregnancy takes a long time though, and while some days are spent joyfully perusing the baby department in John Lewis, the added new emotions and anxieties on both sides, coupled with the huge difference between the man and woman's experience of pregnancy, can mean that there are plenty of other days that are fraught and testing.

PREGNANCY AND YOUR RELATIONSHIP

While us women are witnessing mind-blowing changes both physically and mentally, it's essentially a waiting game for the man. They can be no more than bystanders. When a woman finds out she's pregnant, some things change immediately. Certain foods are off-limits, alcohol is a no-go and, despite your best intentions, you sometimes become a bit of a fun-sponge. Nothing changes for the man, though. He has another nine months before there's any drastic difference to his life and in my more irrational moments this became a bone of contention. Let me give you an example.

As we neared my due date, Charlie suddenly realised that time was ticking and decided that he needed to 'make the most' of being child-free before nights out became a distant memory. I bet this sounds familiar, doesn't it? These occasions would often occur on a Thursday or Friday evening. 'Just a quick drink with the boys,' he would say before promising to be home by 11pm. On most occasions, I would enjoy a quiet night and find it amusing when I'd hear the key in the door at midnight and then a slightly tipsy Charlie trying to convince me that he'd only had 'a couple of pints'. On one particular night, though, and for no particular reason, I lost my shit. I was around 32 weeks pregnant and had had a bad day. Nothing specific, just a bit hormonal. The show that night had been average and I had a jabbing pain just below the ribs, which had exhausted me. I must have been sleeping soundly when Charlie came home because I woke with a start as he leant over the bed to give me a kiss. Despite the gallant gesture, I'm embarrassed to say that instead of just rolling over and going back to sleep, I started ranting about how it was unfair that he could still go out and enjoy himself and why wasn't he home to make supper and look after me? A complete over-reaction.

He turned on his heel and went towards the kitchen to get a glass of water, unwilling to engage. Without missing a beat, I hoisted myself out of bed and followed him, nagging, accusing, wailing as I went. We turned to face each other. He stood there, glass of water in hand, bemused and uninterested. 'Just go to bed, Al.'

It was a red rag to a bull. I was hysterical, now, eyes ablaze and angry. 'You go out cos you don't love me any more.'

Ridiculous. Saying something for the sake of it.

'Al, stop it.'

Me: 'Your life is still normal and I'm stuck here cos I'm too tired to do anything.'

'It was a couple of drinks.'

'You don't fancy me any more!'

Mid-rant, I caught myself in the mirror and stopped dead. I was big, pale and naked, apart from a pair of ill-fitting knickers that were fraying at the seams. I started crying, loud body-shaking sort of crying. I felt ugly, pathetic and regretful about what I'd said. Normally, this would have been the beginning of an explosive row, but Charlie quietly went to get my dressing gown, settled me on the sofa and made me a cup of tea.

Birthing partner

I often wondered what sort of birthing partner Charlie would be. I had a strong inkling that he'd be a good and solid partner, but in fact, he blew that notion out of the water. Charlie was nothing less than outstanding during Teddy's birth. Any relationship niggles we might have had in the last long and frustrating weeks of pregnancy, especially with a house move thrown in, were well and truly forgotten, and I couldn't have been prouder of him the night I gave birth.

He was 100 per cent committed and for ten and a half hours, we locked eyes and he worked with me to bring Teddy safely into the world. He was calm and in control (well, at least from my perspective, which was crouched on all fours) and pre-empted my every want and whim, articulating them assertively when he needed to. I put every inch of my trust in him, often looking to him instead of the midwives for guidance and reassurance. He exceeded my expectations in every sense and the strength and power of the love I felt for him in the aftermath was enormous.

Discussing the delivery

It's a well-known fact that couples worry about the impact witnessing the birth may have on their relationship and we weren't an exception. While some men barely bat an eyelid, others suffer paternal post-partum PTSD. It really is a thing and not to be trivialised.

Before the due date, we had the obligatory chat about which end Charlie would be during the birth and what I was comfortable with him seeing. I was the paranoid one. A misogynistic colleague, who will remain nameless, kept repeating that crude joke about watching your wife give birth being a bit like watching your favourite pub burn down and it bothered me a bit more than it should have.

A big fan of Sir David Attenborough and all things nature, Charlie was unfazed, intrigued even, and keen to buy a front-row ticket, but I wasn't comfortable and he respected my choice. It was a futile conversation anyway, because in the moment: a. I didn't care; b. I was on a bean bag and not in the conventional hospital bed set-up I'd imagined, so everything was a bit more 'exposed'; and c. who could and couldn't see my nether regions was irrelevant. I'm glad I lost my inhibitions because seeing Teddy crown was a unique moment, albeit a hideously excruciating one for me.

Your relationship in the early weeks

> 'What I do know is that it has to be a team effort. In the early days of nappies and feeds it feels like a never-ending cycle with less time for each other, less sleep and the small things like laundry and bath times just feel like they're going to tip you over the edge. Then there's the small moments like out walking with the pram with one child holding your hand without a care in the world and this new baby sleeping so peacefully and you feel such an overwhelming sense of contentment.' Ross

So, in the days following the birth, the three of us were well and truly in the love bubble and everything was looking very rosy, apart from my cheeks, which remained cement-coloured due to extreme blood loss. Charlie had stepped up to the paternal plate in a big way and I couldn't love him more, so how, merely two weeks later, did I want to kill him?

The exasperation, which really did border on hatred for a short spell, started when Charlie returned to work following his statutory paternal leave. Our love bubble had burst with a loud pop and we struggled to find a way to even like each other at some points in those early days. I'm embarrassed to say that we had fallen into the classic trap of arguing pathetically about who was most tired and who had the toughest gig: Charlie, working all day on no sleep, or me, left holding a brand-new baby. I'm still very certain about who wins that one, and I think Charlie agrees deep down, but we've since, for our relationship's sake, let the argument go.

> 'We had the most blissful first two weeks, it was the happiest blur. Then the first morning my husband left at 7.45am for work, and I'm just sitting on the carpet staring at our tiny daughter – you could hear a pin drop! My heart is pumping and I'm thinking, "shit!".' Natalie

It's very well documented how damaging lack of sleep can be to the relationships of new parents, but nothing prepares you for it. This, coupled with the fact that breastfeeding renders the dad almost redundant in those long and endless nights at the beginning of the journey, can make for a very lonely experience for the mother. Charlie, despite his best intentions, would frequently fall into a deep sleep, while I would have to wake at least every two hours to feed our insatiable baby. Some nights I would sit there at 4am, fighting to get Ted to latch on to my ravaged nipple while Charlie snored oblivious next to me. Silent tears would wet Teddy's little crown as loneliness took hold, and on other nights, I would sit there angrily plotting my husband's demise. He was very lucky I had my hands full with a newborn otherwise I may have clonked him over the head with my Medela breast pump!

'We'd never been an argumentative couple, but the sleepless nights drove us almost literally up the wall; we were like two different people.' Rachel

In hindsight, I regret not giving more consideration to how Charlie felt in those first few weeks. He was legitimately knackered, which didn't help, but he also admitted to feeling like a spare part in our new situation. He was sad that while we had been a real team in the hospital, the balance had shifted and it was now all about me and Teddy. He felt pushed out and like the gooseberry in his own family.

I was shell-shocked when Charlie told me that he hadn't bonded with Teddy properly until he was nearly three months. It was a big statement and again I reacted badly. Without stopping to hear his reasons, I jumped to defend Ted, unable to grasp why his dad had felt like this. It turned into a full-blown row, and it was only when Charlie uncharacteristically broke down that I stopped being so self-absorbed and finally listened properly. He explained that he didn't feel that there had been any room or time for him to form as strong a bond as Teddy and I had, and that nearly losing me in the aftermath of the birth had, despite his best efforts, really affected how quickly he could develop that bond with our son because the birth had nearly cost him his wife's life. He had loved his son instantly, of course, but because of what had happened to me, he needed more time than me to feel that indescribable bond that a parent has with their child. It was arrestingly honest and a lot to process, and I didn't know how I felt, apart from relieved that he'd found the strength to admit to such complex feelings. It was a painful conversation, but ultimately, the honesty helped us move forward to a much better place.

THE MUNDANE STUFF

After the first turbulent and testing few months, it was the mundane stuff that was the next hurdle. Five years ago, I never thought we'd be that couple who would waste time arguing over whose turn it was to empty the dishwasher but here we were playing tit for tat, point-scoring for being the last one to put the steriliser on. The messier the house was, the messier our relationship was. In the grand scheme of things, why did I care so much about dirty dishes in the sink or the clean clothes that needed folding and putting away when we were in so much chaos? Unfortunately, though, the background buzz of constant nagging on my part didn't take long to become loud in-your-face tension, which inevitably boiled over, needing us to reassess things once more. The problem is that maintaining a marriage against the backdrop of a new baby takes time and energy, which are the two things you don't have. It's all-consuming.

We found a way through it eventually and you will too if you're prepared to compromise. After much discussion, we agreed that I would simply ask Charlie directly if there were chores that I needed help with and vice versa. Me running about folding laundry and emptying bins while loudly huffing and puffing was getting us nowhere. This straightforward-sounding plan still fails miserably some weeks, but it helps us argue less about the small stuff. Charlie rightly pointed out that it was unlikely that Teddy, in years to come, would remember us as great parents because we regularly emptied the dishwasher and bins. He's got a point.

Charlie was made to be a dad. Unlike me, he's never really known what he wants to do and has fallen into careers rather than choosing them, but I really feel that this is his true calling. He's gentle, entertaining, patient and Ted's hero. I don't even get a look-in when Charlie is in the room, and although I pretend to protest, that's absolutely fine by me. Watching your husband become a brilliant dad is probably the most wonderful thing you will witness. However, I do get a touch irate when he suggests how I should put Teddy down for the night and what his new favourite foods are when I've been away, even for just a couple of days. To be fair, he did wean Teddy off the dummy at night time while I spent a week in Ireland, knowing that I would never manage 20 seconds of hearing Teddy cry. We are team players now; our individual selfishness has been replaced with the shared ideal of becoming the best parents we can be to Teddy.

STRIKING A BALANCE

Striking that balance between being a mum and dad and being a couple is something we still haven't quite mastered. Slowly but surely though we are remembering to make time for each other. Although less intoxicating, there is still a great deal of passion between us, born mostly out of deep respect for how we've both, individually and together, handled the last 18 months, good, bad and everything in between. Like most parents, we have sex half as often and in a sex-or-sleep battle, sleep will always win, but I have no doubt in my mind that having Teddy has been the making of us. The terrible twos or, if we're lucky, a second baby, may go some way to challenging that, but for now, all is well. In fact, it couldn't be better.

'With baby number two things between my husband and me went noticeably downhill. A combination of him working long hours/commuting, me being tired with both a toddler and a newborn and keeping on top of a house work/cooking/ everything else. It was hard. When my youngest was four months old we were barely speaking – we functioned. And at that point I asked for a divorce because it was neither what I wanted, nor could I see a way back - dramatic? Yes but it felt like there was no other option. Thank goodness he could see there was!! There was some shouting, a lot of tears (mainly me!) and a rationality that I didn't have but he did. We're two and a half years on from that – we're not divorced. We love each other and our little family – the lust we once had has turned into a different kind of love and respect for one another – and I guess that's part of growing up and finding our way in life.' Bev

'I got pregnant in summer 2016, unplanned but I was thrilled. By October 2016, I found myself unexpectedly single. I say unexpectedly because I had spent the last three years with a man who made my life a misery but I never left. By 20 weeks and knowing I was bringing another woman into the world, I finally had the strength to leave and never look back. I never wanted her to see or feel my unhappiness. I can't explain the feeling of knowing I was growing my very own new best friend, my reason, my happiness. Since the birth of my beautiful baby girl Poppy in Feb 2017 I have truly learnt how to love. It's been very hard, many tears and confusion but never one ounce of regret. We have a lovely home, a lovely life and we have each other. Poppy's dad has decided not to be involved and I couldn't be more pleased about the fact she is all mine. I am a poster girl for single mamas, the stigma, the questions are horrible but you can triumph. YOU CAN DO IT SINGLE MAMAS!! Winging it doesn't even come close to what I am doing but I am so proud of the both of us. It isn't easy but you can absolutely do it! I've not had one bad day since her arrival, I'm a new woman. Out of my darkness came the brightest light.' Hannah

Sunday strolls

OUR TOP 5
RELATIONSHIP-SAVING TIPS

1

'Communicate, communicate, communicate – it's tempting to bottle up feelings and stew on them, but talking should be an absolute priority, no matter what else is going on: it's imperative that you both know how the other feels.' *Lucy*

'Have had two babies and I know that each time we have a child, our relationship changes in many ways, the biggest issue for me is usually the resentment I feel. Initially after giving birth, a mum's world is thrown upside down, whereas it can seem that the partners life almost carries on as normal. We didn't handle the resentment well and it did nearly cause a break down in the relationship especially after baby number 2. I am expecting our third child next year and I really hope I can learn from the previous two and be more prepared, and hopefully communicate better!' Claire

2

'Talk about your expectations of each other – like, "I would love it if you could please be in charge of bath times" and "I would really like ten minutes to decompress when I get home from work".' *Amelia*

3

'Date nights might sound cheesy, but it is so important to set time aside to be together just the two of you, and to honour those times and not cancel at the last minute.' *Andrew*

4

'Say thank you – gratitude goes a long way.' *Pooja*

5

'Give yourself time to find your new rhythm as parents, and don't put pressure on your relationship to suddenly be the World's Best Parents.' *Guy*

THE REST OF YOUR LIFE?

MOVING PAST THE NEWBORN STAGE —
A TIME OF NEW DISCOVERIES...

THE
TOP 5
MOST ANNOYING
THINGS

YOU'LL HEAR IN THE FIRST YEAR*
*and must just ignore

1 You'd better hurry up with number two

2 That's not a smile, it's just wind

3 My little one will eat anything placed in front of him

4 My child was sitting up at that age

5 You're going back to work so soon? Good for you! I'm going to make the most of this precious time.

THE FOG IS LIFTING

So, you made it through the pandemonium of the first three to four months and, despite moments of self-doubt and some shambolic days, your baby is alive and well. Tick. And your relationship is hopefully still going strong (ish). Tick.

For those of you who are expectant parents, the truth is that it gets a hell of a lot easier from here on in. Normally, feeding is all sorted by now and some parents are even thinking about weaning on to solid food. By four months, your baby can entertain him or herself for short spells instead of having to be attached to you 24/7, and those ten minutes here and there will feel like an all-inclusive week in Sardinia.

The most significant highlight for me at this stage was witnessing Teddy hit his first milestones. Each brought with it unadulterated amounts of happiness and wonder. The first time Teddy rolled over, we whooped and videoed and sent it to all and sundry, then realised that we had become one of *those* sets of parents that we thought we never would be. But who cares? We still can't believe we've managed to make a fully functioning human being. The best moment was knowing for certain that Ted absolutely, 100 per cent recognised *us* as his parents, which was the greatest reward in the world for the blood, sweat and tears that we'd piled into the first few months.

Yes, the mist starts to lift around the 12-week mark. By then, you're in the zone and, for the best part, enjoying being a parent, sleepless nights aside.

> 'My husband started to suffer from anxiety when both our boys arrived, those initial weeks of constant feeding and a lot of crying he just couldn't cope with and his way of dealing with it was to get out of the house. Being honest with each other and talking about how we feel is the only way forward and makes me feel like we have such a close little family with a bond that will only get stronger. I feel truly blessed to have such happy, healthy little boys and as tough as it is at times I wouldn't have it any other way.' Joanna

So, now what? Well, the next bit of tricky terrain, and maybe the hardest of all to navigate, is going back to work, and finding a way for both parents to live the busy lives they had before while factoring in the needs of a young baby.

The average maternity leave in the UK is around nine months – for some it will be longer, for others shorter, depending on each family's circumstances. Deciding factors can sometimes be whether you're employed or self-employed, how flexible your company is, whether you're a single parent or whether you can afford for one of you to stay at home. Whatever your situation, deciding on when to return to work, plus getting your ducks in a row in terms of finding the best and most affordable type of care for your child, is a minefield. My tip would be to start looking at your options early, whether you're both planning to be back at work at three months or a year. Even if your plan is to work from home, meaning you will only need occasional help, you'll probably need to start having those conversations sooner rather than later and plan accordingly, especially if you don't have family living close by.

Like with many other facets of parenting, everybody will offer an opinion based on how long or short your maternity leave is. They'll say things like, 'You're brave to let your husband/partner be a stay-at-home dad', or they might point out that the particular crèche you like that's in your budget isn't 'outstanding' according to Ofsted. Difficult as it can be, you will need to learn to block it all out and do what's right for you.

But, if you're back at work sooner rather than later, then it's not all bad news. It's true that leaving your baby might feel like someone has ripped off your left arm, but work – yes, let's say it out loud – is a break from the relentlessness of child-rearing. The huge benefit is that having a baby gives you perspective, and while the job that you return to may still be as demanding as ever, you will be less likely to get caught up in pointless office politics. From now on, you'll get the job done and get out, because your number one priority is waiting for you at home. It's so refreshing to have that level of clarity.

Your life in some ways will slowly start to resemble the one that you remember pre-baby. Your body will feel like yours again. Most days you'll probably be able to shower before 4.30pm and get a bit of mascara on, which, let's face it, makes the world of difference. The huge bonus is that lots of your pre-maternity clothes will fit, which is like having a whole new wardrobe without having to shell out. Date nights may also be back on the cards and even a night away, which will feel like a sabbatical in the Caribbean.

Parents like us, in our thirties and forties, whose lives were pretty much at capacity before we had a baby, will wonder how on earth we'll fit everything in. Baby, work, deadlines, chores, life admin, a relationship – and all that on little sleep – how will we manage? The amazing thing is that we do. We take solace and strength from the fact that so many others are experiencing the exact same struggles, which I hope is reflected in the next few chapters. The truth of the matter is that you get a lot more done because your focus, out of necessity, becomes a lot sharper. Agreeing to write a book in the first year of having a child as well as trying to hold down a full-time job may have been a step too far, but hey, I'm here and I'm doing it. You'll honestly surprise yourself with what's possible.

'We often have such high expectations of ourselves so try and keep these in check (I know it's really hard). Work out what YOUR priorities are and focus on these things – you can do anything but not everything. The house might be a complete tip, you might need to buy the birthday cake rather than make it, that's o.k, they won't remember it anyway! Focus on quality of time over quantity and know that the guilt thing affects everyone, whether you are at work or not, so be kind to yourself. A good tip for easing the guilt and staying positive is writing down three things you are grateful for at the end of each day. Sometimes for me this was, "had a shower" or "got to work on time" as well as, "the massive cuddle we had on nursery pick up".' Helen, the Guilty Mothers Club, @guiltymother blog

WORK/LIFE HELL

'I found the most difficult thing about going back to work was that no one could adjust to the fact that I was now a parent – it was as though, "well the bump's gone, so you must be able to have that meeting at 7pm, right?"' Paula

It was 8am on a Wednesday. I had a particularly challenging day of work ahead, and was going head first into it after just an hour and a half of sleep the night before. There I stood in front of the full-length mirror in our bedroom, manically rough-drying my hair while Teddy was sitting on the floor, wedged between my legs, entertaining himself by gurgling at his own reflection. He's such a little narcissist, bless him. I was already late, and my cab driver was ringing the doorbell. My phone had rung a couple of times but between the hairdryer and cooing at Teddy I hadn't heard it. As soon as Charlie appeared in a towel from the bathroom to take over, I gave them both a hurried kiss, grabbed my phone and flew down the stairs.

It was only then that I realised that I had four missed calls and two text messages from Jess, who looks after Teddy during the week. She was sorry but she had a high temperature and couldn't make it out of bed. This was totally out of character. Jess is usually so reliable that we always just assume that she will turn up. Shit! To be fair, she'd been under the weather for a couple of days and this was not her fault, but still... SHIT!!

Back upstairs, I quickly explained the situation to Charlie, ending with a firm, 'So, you'll have to have him.'

'What? No! Absolutely not, Al. Not today of all days. I have a meeting with my boss.'

Shit!

'Can't you just go in later?' he offered.

'No, I can't go in later,' I tried to explain patiently. 'The cab is already outside to take me to the voiceover and then we have an extended *One Show* this evening so I really have to be there by 12pm. They'll never get somebody else to present tonight at this short notice!'

Teddy looked at us back and forth like he was watching a tennis match. 'OK, who do we know?'

We ran through a very short list of hopeless options. The obvious saviours would be my parents, but living 210 miles away, they're too far to come to our rescue. I phoned Mum anyway for moral support. She offered to get on a train immediately, which would get her to us by approximately 3pm. Three pm? Shit! Having exhausted every single option, we finally called our NCT teacher Sarah to ask whether she might be available. She wasn't. SHIT! She sensed that these were desperate times and suggested her neighbour's daughter who has done a bit of baby-sitting. We didn't know her from Adam, she could well have been an axe murderer (that was highly unlikely), yet, out of sheer desperation we agreed that that was our only option.

We were both seriously late by the time Hannah, the complete stranger who would be looking after our child for the day, turned up. With tempers frayed and stress levels high, it took every ounce of pretence to look normal and welcoming as we opened the door. My taxi driver was standing just behind Hannah, dragging viciously on his cigarette, the meter running. We stood in the kitchen, trying to make small talk about Hannah's non-existent baby experience, as we decided whether we could risk leaving Teddy with her all day.

As it turned out, she was cleverer than us – an engineering graduate, in fact – and, sensing our fear, she came up with a solution. 'Why don't you take Teddy to work and I'll come with you? That way you can keep an eye on him and tell me exactly what to do, but I'll be there to take him when you need to go to meetings.' I could have kissed her. We had a plan.

> 'My friend once told me, "mums spend 90% of their time feeling guilty and the other 10% asleep". This is so true, if you work you feel guilty for being away from your baby, If you don't work you feel guilty for not contributing financially, if you do both, well you kind of don't win on any front. I even felt guilty at one point for not feeling guilty – I was having so much fun drinking a hot cup of tea at work I hadn't thought about the baby for a few hours, and then felt awful! So know that you are not alone, this is so common.'
> Helen, the Guilty Mothers Club, @guiltymother blog

Having piled the cab with baby equipment, much to the driver's chagrin, off we set. First stop, a massive television company just off Tottenham Court Road in Central London to record a voiceover. Hannah was wide-eyed as we navigated the revolving doors that led us into the impressive glass foyer. The receptionist was less than impressed as she clocked all the baby stuff that was littering her immaculate space. We eventually stuffed everything into the lift and got to the third floor.

Voiceovers and babies are two things that definitely don't mix. While Teddy is as relaxed as they come, he still didn't appreciate having to be absolutely silent while I reeled off the scripted lines as quickly as I could. He wasn't playing ball, and so, nervously, Hannah offered to take him out to the coffee station to let us record in peace. I tried not to worry – it was clear that Hannah was a very sensible young woman – but I just couldn't relax. The quicker I tried to deliver the lines so that I could get back to Ted, the more mistakes I made and the more re-takes were necessary. When I finally got outside the stuffy booth, Hannah looked like she might cry with relief. She was obviously a nervous wreck too.

> 'Because my wife is and was the major wage earner, she had to go back to work after four months. At no time have the girls suffered for not having their mum around and they understand the importance of her job, both professionally and financially. I know my wife sometimes feels very guilty about it, but we have two very healthy, happy and loving girls and that is the most important thing!' Dafydd

Having traipsed through W1 like carthorses, we eventually got to the next stop, *The One Show*. We set up camp in my dressing room and I ran to our meeting, sweating and apologising as I arrived. Back and forth I went between the meeting room and my dressing room, texting instructions to Hannah when I couldn't excuse myself. She'd never even changed a nappy, let alone made up a bottle or dealt with an over-tired child, so every detail needed explaining. She even enlisted the help of one of our guests that evening, Robert Plant from Led Zeppelin, who, to be fair, was more than happy to help. In the meantime, I was completely preoccupied in the meeting. I read the script like Will Ferrell in *Anchorman* and nodded as enthusiastically as I could at various suggestions, having not even heard a word the producers said.

> 'I work full time, finished my masters in 2016 when Bethan, my youngest was less than one. Just finished a huge house project and life is wonderful. After trying a few childcare options we now have a wonderful childminder who works from our home. Absolute best option and would recommend to anyone!' Becky

Make-up was a challenge, with Teddy sat on my lap while Hannah took a well-deserved break. I've never seen anybody bolt so quickly for the door, but thankfully she did come back an hour later for round two. To be fair, the staff at work are absolutely phenomenal and so helpful and the second they heard that Teddy was in the building, the majority of the team descended to offer to take him for a walk. This attitude filters from the top. Our editor is such a supporter of families who are trying to make things work and lets us know that children are always welcome should anybody be hard pushed. It's such a refreshing attitude and we're so lucky to have a boss like him. It was my editor who carried Teddy around the studio while we rehearsed for our live show, but with tiredness creeping in,

Teddy was getting bored of the company of strangers and started to wail uncontrollably for his mother. Shit! Trying to make notes, rewrite questions, read the autocue and soothe Teddy all at once was proving tricky, and all the while, the PA in the gallery counted down to the live show. Minutes before we went live, I saw Charlie running past the window toward the studio to take over, like Batman through the mist. The studio light turned red and the titles started playing. I passed Ted to Charlie and got back on the sofa just in time to say, 'Hello and welcome to *The One Show*', sitting on his dummy as I made contact with the sofa.

What a day! I was exhausted, not to mention poor Hannah, who looked shell-shocked. After an obligatory photo of Ted, Charlie and his idol Robert Plant, which made the entire nightmare a lot more palatable, we eventually got a very tired Ted into the cab and the four of us made our way home. It was my first experience of truly winging it as a working parent and, goodness knows, it was an eye opener, especially the realisation that when the shit had hit the fan, we had very few people who we could turn to for support.

Our situation is typical of so many parents in their thirties and forties who are trying to juggle a demanding job with raising a baby without help at hand. Our coping methods are different to those of our parents' generation. Back then, of course, generally speaking, men went to work and women stayed at home to care for the children, but in a world where us women are financially independent, equally or more ambitious than the men, and sometimes the main breadwinners of the household, things are far more complicated.

We are the first generation to rip up the rulebook and do it our own way, finding ways to make the situation work for both parents. It's far from easy though. In fact it's impossible on some days, and the pace of life can become unbearably relentless as you try to be as present as possible at home and at work. The much-talked-about work–life balance is most often a myth, but it can be made more manageable by getting the right care in place, plus, as we learnt the hard way, some backup care.

WHEN D DAY ARRIVED

On my very last day of maternity leave, Teddy and I took a long walk to our favourite park, enjoying the spring sunshine. I sat feeding him in the cafe where we'd spent many happy afternoons over the previous three months, and I felt intensely sad. It was as if I could hear every second counting down before I had to transform from full-time mother to working mother. It felt too soon to be leaving my brand-new son, but months ago I'd made unrealistic and uninformed promises about when I'd return to work, and despite stalling the starting date by a fortnight, it had still come around way too soon. I looked down at Ted, contentedly feeding with no idea that he would be handed over to a virtual stranger the next morning. He looked tiny, helpless and I felt like a shambles of a mother.

Whether it's three, six, nine months or even a year before you return, it's unlikely that any of us will feel truly ready to go back to work. Although social and workplace attitudes towards combining a family and a career have improved, I feel that there is still an outdated stigma that surrounds 'working mothers'. What's staggering about that is that there are **4.9 million working mothers in the UK, a rise of 1.2 million in the last decade**, and while new childcare policies and work practices, including a progressively better attitude towards paternal leave, go some way to explaining the rise, in most cases mothers work because it's necessary. These days, it takes two salaries to raise a family, yet, incredibly, we are still branded as selfish, ambitious, unloving and unreliable. Thanks. What we really are is nothing short of wonder women, achieving the impossible on a daily basis, and nurturing children who will benefit by watching strong and successful mothers and follow in their footsteps.

As wonderful as that sounds, and although it's true, I fear nothing will ever quash those feelings of guilt that are experienced by working mothers across the world every hour of every day. The only comfort, I suppose, is knowing that we all feel the same. Guilt has plagued me, and continues to do so every single day that I put on my coat and kiss Teddy goodbye. It's worse now at nine months when he realises that I'm about to leave and every time, without fail, his little face crumples as if the end of the world is nigh. I can only imagine how hard it must be once they're able to articulate that they're upset.

I can try to convince myself that by working I'm securing a better future for my son, but in my heart of hearts, I know that all he wants, particularly over the next few years, is my time, which costs absolutely nothing. It's a hard realisation to cope with.

So why do I work? Well, firstly, because I need to, and secondly, because I want to. There, I've said it.

Women who become mothers still have needs. Yes, we are head over heels in love with our baby, but it's OK to value the career that we have worked bloody hard to build and to want to continue to enjoy. Some of us also want to be financially independent. When we become mothers we automatically place our needs second to our baby, but we are still allowed to have wants, and whether we want to stay at home or continue with a career that we love, the choice is ours.

Mothers who decide to stay at home rarely get it any easier than working mums. Nurturing a child is still, to a degree, seen as squandering the time and talent of an educated woman when, in fact, it's the hardest and most important job of all, and one that I for one would struggle to do every single day. I need to go away to appreciate family life when I come home, days off and weekends are now sacred, but some women who have come to motherhood later, feel that they have done their time out in the field and want to fully embrace being a parent.

For others, the decision to stay at home may be dictated by the soaring costs of childcare making it financially pointless for both parents to return to the workplace.

Whatever your scenario, just have faith and confidence in the fact that you have tried to make the best choices for your family and crack on. It's all you can do.

MY CAREER

I've always been healthily ambitious. Even as a painfully shy and awkward 11-year-old girl from West Wales, I had big dreams. I was conscientious at school and worked hard. My parents instilled a very strong work ethic, but I put a lot of pressure on myself to achieve and my mum and dad would often have to force me to put my books away and go to bed at exam time. I know, what a swot, but I knew that it would take an extraordinary amount of effort to get me to where I wanted to be and I was quietly focused.

Fast forward 20 years and I'm exactly where I wanted to be, mostly due to sheer determination and perseverance, and partly due to luck. I spent years and years learning my craft as a presenter, working on children's programmes for the first eight years of my career before graduating to more grown-up fare like a holiday show, some sport programmes, a fashion programme; I even dabbled in poker programmes at one point. It was a mixed bag, but luckily the ground work had been done and when, out of the blue, I had a phone call from the deputy editor of *The One Show* in June 2010 who asked me to come and audition, I was ready. It felt right from that first conversation and after six long and rigorous weeks of auditions, the job was finally mine.

I was in Brighton, fronting a skateboarding competition (I told you it was varied), when the good news came. I was to keep it very hush-hush and was only allowed to tell my parents and sister. I immediately rang Mum, who was at work.

'Right. Promise not to tell anybody...'

'Promise!'

Deep breath. 'I got the job!'

'She got the job!' she shouted across the banking hall.

So much for keeping it quiet. The next few weeks were

a whirlwind. Adrian Chiles and Christine Bleakley left *The One Show* and Jason Manford and I, before the days of Matt Baker, were to be the new pairing on the green sofa. My life was suddenly unrecognisable. Paparazzi would follow me, trying desperately to piece together a picture of 'this girl' who had seemingly come from nowhere to present the BBC's flagship nightly programme. I can only imagine that the feeling was akin to winning *The X Factor*. It was zero to a hundred. Suddenly, days were filled to the brim with interviews and photoshoots and journalists were camped on my parents' drive. I was thrilled about the job – it was the one I had wanted forever and I felt confident that I would do a good job, but what I wasn't prepared for was the circus that came with it.

The first night on air was a heart-stopping, nerve-racking affair. There was so much riding on it.

Whoopi Goldberg, who was starring in the new production of *Sister Act* in the West End, was the guest. In true *One Show* style, we also had an item on the re-introduction of beavers to the rivers of Scotland, and so there was no escaping the word beaver and the hilarity that ensued. It seems very childish now, looking back. I put it down to nerves.

Anyway, that debut happened seven years ago, and I am still overjoyed every single day to be sitting on that very same sofa. I'm incredibly lucky to have one of the most constant jobs in what is a notoriously fickle and competitive industry.

Before I announced that we were expecting a baby, some people assumed that I must have decided to forego having children in favour of a high-profile career. It's an assumption that's often made when a thirty-something female hasn't procreated, but you and I know that there are a million reasons for this, none of which should necessarily hinge on a career. While I love and wholeheartedly appreciate my career, it would never win in a battle with having a family of my own, never in a million years, but having said that, I admit that I did have my share of worries and paranoia about having to disappear on maternity leave.

I was thrilled to be pregnant, but scared of having to let go, and I will freely admit that the thought of seeing someone else in my seat on *The One Show* filled me with horrible feelings of dread and jealousy. Show me a successful career woman who is about to turn new mother who denies having any such thoughts about her maternity leave, and I will show you a liar.

So, after 14 weeks, I went back to work. My life had changed exponentially, but at *The One Show* everything was as it always had been and the familiarity was comforting. I was nervous and felt like the new girl all over again but as I sat on the sofa, the butterflies gradually disappeared as Matt, my co-presenter, and I relaxed back into our familiar roles. It was as if no time had passed; the only difference was that I had breast pads under my dress and I was a bit chubbier than I had once been, but even that evening's black dress went some way to disguising that.

At the end of the first day, I rang my parents, as I always do after a show.

'So, how was it?' asked Dad.

'Good,' I answered. 'Actually, it was fun to be back.'

It had felt like a break. It didn't compare to being with

Teddy in the slightest, but it had been quite nice to be able to do things with both hands, to have a cup of tea and actually drink it, to go to the toilet when I felt like it without having to plan, to have a chat with friends I hadn't seen for ages, to put some make-up on and to wear something other than jogging bottoms, to wear a proper bra that actually did the job, to engage my brain and remember that thing that I was good at and enjoyed doing before I became a mother, to prove to myself that I could in fact be a mother and have a career. The thing that had felt impossible was possible and, what's more, here I was doing it. It felt like a victory.

The best bit of that day was yet to come. After what felt like the longest journey home, I finally had my little boy back in my arms where he belonged. He and I had survived the first day.

Having said that, some weeks, especially at the very beginning, were nothing less than horrific. It was about a fortnight after returning to work and the shine of being back had naturally begun to wear off. Teddy was coming up to the four-month mark and the much-talked-about 'sleep regression' had kicked in. Suddenly, we went from sleeping seven hours a night to being woken five or six times and he would want to feed at least twice. We were back to a routine that echoed the early days when we'd just brought him home from the hospital, except this time, instead of being able to spend the following day at home, I'd have the morning at home with Ted and then, with red-rimmed eyes and sallow skin, would be live on the television come seven o'clock. I'd get home at eight and the whole process would start again. That's the thing: after coming home from a day in the trenches, instead of a glass of wine and some telly, you then must deal with a cranky and clingy baby, which is often far more challenging than the day job.

The support at work had been unwavering for the whole of my pregnancy and maternity leave yet, human nature meant that, without the visual aid of a bump, colleagues soon forgot.

There were no excuses or exceptions made for the fact that I was coping with a tiny human, that I had no downtime, let alone sleep, and that my nerves, patience and tolerance levels were in shreds. My usual sense of humour had abandoned ship, meaning that every slight negative comment or remark cut to the core, leaving me feeling vulnerable and incapable. Added to the mix was the fact that I was trying to pump the living daylights out of each breast between meetings so that I could live up to the ridiculous standards that I set for myself of keeping Ted on breast milk despite me being back at work. That week I felt I was a crap mother and a crap presenter. No one was winning, least of all me.

> 'I really struggled with going back to work; I felt like I was trying to do the same job on half a brain and even less sleep – I felt guilt that I wasn't with my baby, and guilt that I hadn't sufficiently "bounced back".' Aoife

The problem with society these days is that women who do 'bounce back' and are at their desks within days of giving birth are celebrated, putting an inordinate amount of pressure on the rest of us. Part of me wants to applaud these women like Rachida Dati, the former French minister who was famously pictured tottering down the road in heels just five days after her caesarean, but another part of me wants to scream at them, 'WHAT ARE YOU DOING?' The gravitas of childbirth, emotionally, spiritually and physically, has been quashed somewhat, and we are being slowly brainwashed, especially by the media, to think that our goal should be to be back to 'normal' or back at work quicker than you can get your pyjama bottoms back on after labour. I'm all for an 'I can' attitude, but in the aftermath of labour we need to give each other time. Instead, we are getting caught up in this unrealistic fast-moving current.

I cried every night during my first week back at work. Well, it wasn't just the nights. I cried in the shower in the morning, I cried at the back door as I left Ted, then some more in the car on the way to work while I spoke to Mum, a bit in my dressing room as I desperately tried to fit into something, anything, on the clothes rail where my pre-pregnancy clothes hung. Then, I'd cry a bit more once I was in the car on the way home after another catastrophic performance and so on and so on. It just wasn't me. The strong, capable person I really am was missing in action. The good news is that nobody else at work had an inkling, and after the first couple of weeks, I hit my stride and it got a bit better each day. Slowly but surely, your confidence comes back, you get used to the tiredness, the weight shifts a bit, and you find your rhythm.

WORKING AWAY

So what about those men and women who have to travel for work? For them, I have the utmost respect. It's downright bloody hard. My biggest challenge to date was the aforementioned week away in Northern Ireland when *The One Show* went on the road for a week in the summer. Four whole nights without your baby at that stage feels like losing a limb. Leaving Ted on that Monday morning was a killer. I clearly remember the conversation between Mum and me as I shut the taxi door.

'Hi, Al,' she answered chirpily.

'Hiya.' The lump in my throat made my voice small and weak.

'You're on your way, are you?'

My voice completely broke and the tears that had threatened to spill as I said goodbye to Teddy in his cot came flooding out. The driver looked in his rear-view mirror and gave me a sympathetic smile.

'You'll be back in no time, Al,' assured Mum.

'I know,' I said, and didn't believe a word of it.

So there I stood in Terminal 2, with red eyes and blotchy skin (I've just realised how much crying I did), feeling incredibly guilty that I was going AWOL for a whole week. I wondered whether Teddy would remember me when I got back. What if he woke at night crying out for me? I knew that Ted would be cared for brilliantly by Jess during the day and Charlie at night, but horrendously and selfishly, there was a dark side of me that wanted Ted to wonder where his mama was, and to recognise that I wasn't there and to damn well be upset about it. It was a real dilemma.

Again, we both survived, saved mostly by FaceTime and a husband who stepped up to the plate and fathered like he'd never fathered before.

That week, after sniffling all the way to Heathrow, I gave myself a good talking to, and decided that the best way to deal with the situation was to accept that I couldn't be in two places at once and therefore I was going to embrace the week ahead, there was no other option so I might as well get on and commit to it. It turns out that it's always better to be fully present somewhere as opposed to nowhere.

The thing with working away, and I'm loath to admit it, especially to Charlie, who already suspects that parts of it are a bit of a jolly, is that you get to do things that you simply can't with a baby, for example, dinners in restaurants, long showers or even baths, uninterrupted breakfasts and the big one – sleep.

But the biggest benefit of working away is the welcome you receive once you arrive home. After Northern Ireland, I ran breathless through the door and upstairs to Teddy's nursery just as he was about to go down for the night. The second he saw me, his whining stopped, and slowly but surely the widest smile spread across his little face, and as I put my face closer to the cot to breathe in that indescribably delicious baby smell, up came his little fists to gently touch my face. I thought that my heart would explode there and then. I've genuinely never felt love as intensely. We locked eyes, smiling broadly at each other. He felt like home.

Heading back to work

Dare I say it, the biggest worry that haunts you during the early days is whether your baby loves the person looking after her or him more than you. It sounds pathetic, and I know it's a bit controversial because rarely does anybody say it out loud, but come on, we've all felt it. I suppose it's a mix of jealousy and envy that they're with your child and you're not. It particularly hurts when they are the ones who end up having to take your child to the GP; that feels like the pits.

Our nanny Jess is wonderful in so many ways and I never, ever want her to leave. We would be royally screwed without her, but knowing that Teddy doesn't want to let *me* go in the morning and behaves like Christmas has come early every time I come home fills my heart with joy. Us parents will always be number one, so that is one thing less to sweat about, and it does feel like such a privilege to be that most important and vital person in his life despite not being with him 24/7.

So if you're going back to work after three, six, nine or 12 months, try not to build it up too much. Remember that things are unlikely to have changed that much, and even if they have, it's nothing that a woman who has just navigated childbirth and bringing up a baby can't deal with. Remember that studies also prove that working mothers often outperform other women. As mums, we, by necessity, acquire and perfect a whole range of employable skills and qualities in the first year of our new little human's life, so even if you're looking for a new challenge that's more flexible, and can fit around your family, don't panic, because you are way more employable now than you were pre-baby. It's all about knowing how to transfer those newly learnt skills – like planning, prioritising, time management, crisis management – to your new or current job and using them to your advantage. The sky's your limit!

'I used to be a fashion journalist so I feel as if running a brand is like sitting on the other side of the fence: once I interviewed people about their brands, and now I run one! The progression was very natural though, as Selfish Mother started as a blogzine where I wrote about my experience of motherhood. I created it while still working as a freelance journalist and when it took off I simply wrote less and less articles for other people. Selfish Mother the blog now has 4,000 writers! Don't think of making an adjustment to your previous profession as a career-change as that could be a bit scary, instead think of it as a new way to use your skill set. Work out what your skills are and how you could use them in a new way. Think of it as your natural next step and you will feel more empowered!' Selfish Mother

Most days, all I want to do is be with Teddy – spend the morning at a playgroup, then in the afternoon hang out with my other mum friends and their babies in Pain Quotidien, stuffing an almond croissant down my throat and throwing back my second Americano. As we all know, though, that is not always all it's cracked up to be either, especially when your nine-month-old has decided to single-handedly bring the place down by knocking over every goddamn item on the table, throwing the contents of his Ella's kitchen pouch at any passing customer and, over-tired and in desperate need of a nap, having the mother of all tantrums as you try to wrangle him into the pram.

It's OK to admit that some days, especially after a slog of a night when your eardrums have had a hammering, it's a relief to be able to remove yourself from the situation and swap it for work, where you're in control and feel confident. It's nigh on impossible to strike a good balance. You'll have periods when you feel that you're nailing it, and periods when you feel that you're falling apart, but in those difficult periods remember that you are part of an army, an army of five million other working mothers in the UK who are also doing their best just to get through the day. I'm very proud to be one of them.

'I have severe endometriosis and was told for years that I wouldn't have children. I'm 32 and my miracle, precious boy is now seven months. I'm going back to work in two weeks : I only got statutory mat pay, so staying off for longer is just not possible. I am logical, driven and ambitious, so I thought going back to work would be fine and that I had it all planned. Now, as I prepare to start, I'm a mess. I'm torn between what's best for my baby and what's best for my emotions and selfishness. After a lot of talking, we're now splitting the care between our sets of grandparents. I have struggled with letting go and allowing them to help or care. I also feel that it is important, fair and in Harry's best interests to integrate him with other children and adults who are not in his closest circle, so when he turns one, I intend to put him into nursery for two mornings, I have also now secured flexible working, which will allow me to work from home two days, I will not keep Harry with me these full days, but it will allow me to cut out travel time, eat meals with him and still maintain my full-time hours. I feel that it is important for Harry to see me working and although I would love to spend every waking moment with him and hold him close to me forever, that is not fair on him and so many other people love him and are good for him. Also, the world can be scary, but if I don't expose him to it, how can he survive it? Everyone is different and although these are my choices, if parenthood has taught me anything, it is, nobody has all the answers, we're all in it together and hopefully we all get there.' Frances

HITTING THOSE MILESTONES... YOURS & THEIRS

These markers can send even the most pragmatic parent into a spin. Smiling, rolling, eating, crawling, teething, walking – the first glimpse of each new stage of development is magic as you watch your little human take shape. Like your own personal episode of *Planet Earth*, you observe your baby closely, looking for signs of change, mesmerised by every new noise and movement, and you become obsessed with recording and documenting each milestone on your phone. I could single-handedly fill the entire iCloud with footage and photos of Teddy. There are hundreds of them, all sitting in my iPhone's memory, because there's never any time to get to Snappy Snaps, print some out and stick them in a frame. I used to waste an extraordinary amount of time on Instagram and the *Daily Mail* app, but these days my preferred procrastination activity is swiping through photos of my Ted, sometimes nostalgically going right back to 22 January 2017, his first day on the planet, and marvelling at how he's slowly morphing into a little boy. Time really is zipping by.

THE FIRST SMILE

One of the first, and the most memorable, milestones is your baby's first smile. Ours happened exactly three weeks after Ted was born. I was standing in the kitchen, holding him in my arms after a particularly torturous feeding session that ended in tears on both sides, and as if by way of apology he looked up at me and gave me his first proper, gummy smile. My heart flipped. The irony was that I was so delighted that I shouted at Charlie to come and see, and in the process frightened the life out of Teddy and reduced him to tears.

Now, according to the numerous baby developmental apps that clog up my home screen, you can expect your baby's first smile any time between six and 12 weeks. Before then, according to those who are apparently in the know, it's likely to be your baby's reflex smile, or wind to you and me. I'm no expert, but I know what I saw, and there's a big difference between a 'windy' smile and a 'proper' smile. For weeks, when Teddy smiled, people would patronisingly say, 'Oh, look, he's got a bit of wind' and I silently wanted to punch them, knowing that Ted had already nailed smiling. Trust your instinct: you're the parent, you'll know it when you see it.

MY MAJOR MILESTONE

At seven weeks, according to the app, Teddy's focus would be sharper, he'd really start to enjoy looking at black-and-white images, he'd begin to open and close his little fists, his movements would be less jerky and more purposeful as he lost his newborn reflexes and his sleeping habits would become a little more predictable. HOORAY! While those were his milestones, in the same week I was hitting a big one of my own: my fortieth birthday.

Back in my twenties, I would never have imagined that I would turn 40 just weeks after giving birth to my first child. Back then, I assumed that 40 was ancient, and that I'd be closer to waving my children off to uni by now. That, however, is not how the story went, and actually, I like this version a lot better. I have no idea how 40 happened though. I mean, of course I do, but it's crept up on me like a stealthy fox. One minute I was 26 and the next, here I am, halfway to 80! As someone who dreaded their thirtieth, I was surprised that I didn't feel anything but ease as I crossed the border into my fifth decade. It might have been down to the hormones, the leftover oxytocin after labour, but it felt nothing but celebratory. I was exactly where I wanted to be in life, and Teddy arriving on the cusp of the big birthday was the icing on the (birthday) cake.

My only issue with turning 40 was the pressure to celebrate the occasion. I wasn't ready for a night out, especially without Ted. A big part of me wanted to postpone it until I'd had more than two hours of continuous sleep, until my boobs had stopped leaking, until I could potentially fit into something that was worthy of a fortieth birthday party and until I was certain that I could drink more than one glass of champagne without collapsing in an embarrassing heap. However, time waits for no woman, and it seemed ridiculous not to mark the occasion. So after some persuasion - and a giant online order from Zara, just to make sure that I'd have something to wear - we settled on some drinks at home with close friends and then a low-key dinner for 35 while Mum and Dad looked after Ted. Nice and civilised.

It was 18 March 2017, 11.30pm. We were done at the restaurant after a raucous supper and, having flagged down eight taxis, were en route to our favourite dancing venue in Soho for more champagne and shenanigans. It was my fortieth, after all, and despite not having a drink for nearly a year, I was, surprisingly, upright. At 3.30am, we decided that we still hadn't enjoyed ourselves quite enough, so it was then back to one of the hotels where some of the visiting Welsh crowd were staying. We all piled into one bedroom and turned the music up loud before cracking open the minibar. Before I could take my first sip of the ropey white wine, I'm disappointed to report, I passed out on the bed, letting my friends party around me. The demands of mothering a small baby had finally caught up with me, but hey, I'd put in a good shift and given it my all.

This is 40!

Needless to say, the next morning was sheer hell. The combination of pounding headache, dry mouth and very painful boobs, having not expressed for 12 hours, was threatening to tip me over the edge. Forget 40, I felt and looked 90! Mum and Dad rose to the challenge, as they always do, making masses of spaghetti bolognaise for everybody who called at the house to say goodbye before hitting the M4 on their way back to Wales. I could hardly lift my head from the sofa and only managed to sit upright long enough to 'pump and dump' to make sure that all the alcohol was out of my system before I could start feeding Ted again. A lot of breast milk saw the bottom of the sink! The day passed in a fog and, as we eventually staggered up to bed at 11pm having given Ted

Mam and Dad meeting the grandson for the first time

a feed, we wondered what sort of night was in store for us; the thought of waking every few hours was nearly too much to bear. We popped Ted in his crib and gratefully climbed into bed, desperate for sleep.

Teddy's usual snuffling did wake me as it always did, but feeling surprisingly refreshed, I pressed the display on my phone to check the time: 6am. Hallelujah!! Little Ted had slept right through the night for the first time, giving me the best birthday present I could have asked for. It was as if he'd sensed our desperation for sleep and decided to give us a break. Another milestone that called for its own celebration.

CELEBRATING YOUR PERSONAL MILESTONES

As well as your baby's milestones, it's just as important to plan towards your own, and not just the big ones like turning 40. The mundane ones, like the first time you manage to have your hair cut after having your baby, deserve a cheer, and your first bikini wax warrants an even bigger one. Just a note on that: the first is the worst. Hold on tightly to the bed, grit your teeth and remember how good it will feel to be able to walk around in your underwear again without looking like someone's toupee has fallen into your knickers.

Then there's the bigger stuff – planning your first night out as a couple. I would suggest that this should be mandatory at three months, if not before. You need time to remember what it was like to be a couple and why you liked each other in the first place. With a bit of forward planning, you can find a suitable baby-sitter, just for a couple of hours, or rope in the grandparents. It really doesn't have to be more than a quick bite to eat in your local pub, but having some one-on-one time resets everything and you will face the next baby battle united and therefore stronger.

Our local is so close that our baby monitor could pick up a signal from there at a push. We walked in on our first night, baby-free, to a warm welcome from the landlady, who was visibly delighted to see two of her best customers return after a hiatus of about ten months. (Their profits had probably diminished somewhat in that time.) The first sip of red felt like nectar from the gods, the food was delicious and the conversation sparky and flirty, but we both knew that there was an elephant in the snug. Charlie carefully broached the subject: 'It's a bit weird without Ted, isn't it?' It opened the floodgates and we spent the rest of the evening gushing about our baby. It's what parents do, as it turns out, but it was healthy to have those couple of hours to reflect, reset and then start all over again.

'I'll never forget our first date night, minus tiny person. We went to the cinema and left after the first 40 minutes, we just couldn't concentrate on anything other than Toby! It did make us realise that we'd have to make a proper effort though; time together is still paramount.' Chris

GETTING FRUSTRATED

Between five and six months we started to notice some more significant developments in Teddy. Rolling over was the first biggie, which seemed to take him an age to master. We would make sure he had plenty of 'tummy time', as suggested, but nothing was happening. He couldn't quite muster enough momentum to completely flip over, and that resulted in some pretty fiery tantrums by day and many long nights, as his desire to accomplish this, coupled with his brain development, started to hinder his sleep. Some nights we would be back and forth across the landing more times than we could count, finding Teddy face down in the cot, having rolled and got stuck halfway. We would then have to turn him back over, just to repeat the same process ten minutes later. Whatever stage your baby is at, or whatever their focus is, be it rolling or crawling, we quickly learnt that the nights definitely get a bit more... shall we say *interesting* when your baby is trying to master something new. It's bloody frustrating, but what can you do?

WEANING EN FRANCE

Just before Teddy turned six months, we took our first summer holiday, to France. Naturally, this meant tons of new experiences:

his first plane ride, his first taste of very hot weather (which came with its own challenges) and his first time in a swimming pool. Obviously, I have 573 pictures, to be precise, documenting the whole lot. The major milestone though was having his first taste of proper food, although we hadn't really planned it that way.

Now, there is nothing worse than when someone is staring at a plate of food that you've ordered at a restaurant. A classic case of food envy. You feel obliged to ask whether they would like to try some, when actually you really don't mean it. They tend to look at you expectantly as you lift each forkful to your mouth. My husband is very guilty of this. He will ask as casually as he can, eyes never moving from the plate, whether I'm enjoying it. 'Mmmmm,' I'll answer non-committally, knowing that he wants more detail. 'Nice, is it?', he persists. I nod, mouth full, wanting to savour the taste. One last go on his part. 'Wow, you're enjoying that, aren't you?' I give in and grudgingly offer the much-anticipated forkful.

If you want to know when your baby is ready to move on to solids, it will be a similar experience. When straightforward milk has lost its shine, and your baby is over it, you will know. They will eye up absolutely everything that you put in your mouth and you will start to feel guilty. Often, I'd stand with my head in the kitchen cupboard after work, shovelling down three or four crackers at a time so that Ted wouldn't see me. The longing in his eyes was too much. I think that I probably could have started him on solids earlier than I did, but there were three main reasons stopping me: a. the advice on most websites, including the NHS, that recommends waiting until the six-month mark or until your baby can sit up unaided; b. I literally didn't know where to start; c. we had just had a new kitchen put in and I wasn't ready for it to be covered in carrot purée. Milk feeds were confined, neat and simple.

That small respite between breastfeeding and solids is heaven. Five formula feeds a day, every three hours, is as straightforward as it gets, but just a month into that regime and Teddy was ready for the solid stuff. He was five months when he really started showing an interest. Eating his fists and dribbling had started way before this, but I had just put that down to teething. In fact, once Teddy was older than three months I blamed everything on teething – writing this now, with Ted at nearly ten months, there is still no sign of a tooth... but hey.

So where to start? I bought a couple of books and learnt about the differences between normal weaning and baby-led weaning. Don't be alarmed; this basically means **feeding them with a spoon (normal weaning) or letting your baby pick stuff up with their hands (baby-led weaning)**. It depends on how keen you are to know what quantities they're eating, and how much mess you can handle.

> 'We tried the baby-led weaning route, and as joyful as it was to see Hattie's eyes light up at a plate of mashed sweet potato, I will never get the hours spent cleaning it up from under the fridge back!' Carrie

I decided that we would do a combination. Some purée and some finger bits – after all, that's how we all eat even as adults, isn't it? Sometimes with cutlery and sometimes not. Beyond that, I had no plan. I would just see how things would pan out and put the whole thing off for as long as possible. I was hoping that we could start after we came back from France. I hoped that we could stick to the simple and straightforward milk routine for the holiday and then think about batch cooking, freezing and finding a giant plastic sheet to protect the kitchen on our return. Teddy, on the other hand, had very different ideas.

In the first few days of that holiday, we saw Ted transform. It may have been the hot weather or the fact that suddenly he had our undivided attention 24 hours a day, but gone was the baby who would happily lie quietly in his pram and in his place was a social animal, into everything, and up for trying anything new. Food was right at the top of his agenda, much like his dad. He would eyeball us at the dinner table and it became impossible to eat with him on our laps as we had been doing because he would yank any plate or glass towards him, mouth dribbling, eyes wide. He looked with such longing at the endless variety of food that we were eating, and so I caved.

The plan of waiting to wean was simply unrealistic; this little boy was over milk and was ready to start his gastronomic journey. Bugger! I riffled through the basic cupboards of the house where we were staying, looking for a blender or a food processor. Nothing. I had read that you needed to blitz up carrots and sweet potato and freeze in ice cube trays so that you could feed the baby a couple of squares at a time. Good idea, but here in our rustic house in the middle of a very rural village in France, all my plans to blitz just organic veg and fruit, and to make a lovely chart that we would stick on the kitchen wall noting Ted's likes and dislikes, were not to be. Instead at the local Intermarche, I clumsily read some labels in my pidgin French and gave in at the first hurdle and bought three pots of already prepared puréed veg: carottes, haricots vert and pommes de terre, my Mother Earth ideals up in smoke before my very eyes.

That evening after his last milk feed, Teddy had his first taste of real food; (well, hang on, that's a lie because on our day out at the zoo I gave him a bit of my strawberry Mini-Milk, which he loved, and before the complaints start, I agree that it wasn't the best place to start).

First up was carrot. Tentatively, I raised it towards his mouth and he met my hand halfway and dragged it with a strength that was just bizarre for a baby into his gaping mouth. It was a feeding frenzy until the plastic bowl had been scraped clean. He couldn't get it down fast enough. There was no sign of the food escaping and dribbling down the side of the mouth, which I expected, especially right at the beginning. Spoonful after spoonful disappeared into his eager little mouth with as little as he could manage being wasted. It was the best day of his life so far! I then started giving him bits of veg and fruit in nets that he could chew on. That was a less messy way of deciphering what tastes he enjoyed, plus it was a great toy and he felt like he was joining in when us adults were having a snack. Just a note though, banana brought the life of the net to a premature end as you just can't get it clean after that.

It turned out that Ted liked everything, with the exception of cucumber, but that's fair enough. His dad can take or leave that too. Within days he was refusing his milk and was happily getting through half a glass jar of purée at a time. I was head to toe covered in orange goo and kept finding unpleasant lumps of purée in all sorts of crevices. So much for the lovely white linen cover-ups that I'd planned to wear poolside – they were quickly saturated with sloppy vegetables, but the pleasure that was so evident on Ted's face made it absolutely worth it. Thank goodness for stain remover. When you start to wean, you will need litres of the stuff.

Getting to grips with weaning

Weaning Ted wasn't as we planned or expected, yet it all fell into place at exactly the right time. The three of us being together on holiday meant that we could share that special experience. Watching your child start to experiment with flavours and textures is one of the most satisfying and interesting milestones of the first six months, and we were so glad that we got to do it as a family. Charlie and I were both present at every mealtime during the first fortnight to witness his first reaction to every flavour we offered. It was without a doubt one of the highlights of the holiday, so with that in mind, my advice would be this: don't stress too much about the preparation and don't overthink how 'organic' everything should be. Of course, it's important to give them the best ingredients you can, but keep it simple. Buy a pouch or a jar if you need to and don't beat yourself up about it. Wait until you absolutely think that your baby is ready and then they'll be excited about experimenting and it will be pleasurable all round. Consider doing it on holiday as this means you can enjoy the process together, and the big bonus, you can take the very messy task outside and hose the remnants away. Take your baby's lead and savour the experience. And one last thing: take loads of photos; they're gold and will be priceless on his or her eighteenth birthday.

When we got home, Charlie (a chef by trade) took great pleasure in whizzing up some home-made purées, moving on to more complex recipes as Ted got older. He quickly got bored of bland combinations, and with the help of a few really good weaning recipe books and some very low-salt Kallo stock cubes to add a bit more depth of flavour, Ted ate like a king. By eight months he was dropping most daytime milk feeds in favour of solids and I simply followed his lead. I still really appreciate those morning

Weaning time at the zoo!

and evening feeds as it's the only time he still resembles a young baby. At only nine and a half months he's eating us out of house and home so I dread to think what he'll be like by the time he hits his teenage years. His squidgy thighs are humongous and people keep saying how he'll lose the weight once he starts walking, but for me, he's perfect just the way he is.

'I work full time and have two boys (aged 4 and 2). Multitasking like a mother is the only way to get through! Cleaning the bathroom while the kids are in the bath; cleaning the bath when I'm in the bath (!); making the boys' packed lunch while I make the tea. I've learned to lower my standards big style when it comes to housework – who cares there are creases in our clothes, handmarks on the windows, dust on the skirting boards – plenty of time for housework when the birds have flown the nest! Oh and wipes - wipes clean everything - bums, dashboards, faces, carpets!' Priti

BETH BENTLEY
Founder of baby weaning online platform @Young_Gums

The one thing I wish I'd known before I started weaning my baby was: consider the week, not the day.

During weaning a baby's appetite can fluctuate wildly, affected by teething, tiredness, little sickness bugs, routine changes, growth spurts and more. It's normal. But in the moment, seeing your baby refuse food can be worrying, especially if it continues for several mealtimes. The nutritionist I check my Instagram recipes with told me: *consider the week, not the day.* If you think about all the foods your baby's encountered over the past week you'd probably be surprised at just how widely – and how much – they've eaten. Until around the first birthday, milk remains the main nutrition-source, so even when a meal ends up anywhere but the baby's mouth it's very unlikely he or she will be hungry (and babies know how to let us know they're hungry!). This perspective-shift helps me feel more philosophical about the whole thing, and it's the advice I always pass on to other new parents.

There is so much conflicting weaning advice out there, and it's easy to get bogged down in what can feel like an endless battle to just get food in mouth. But babies will pick up on panicked vibes, so although its easier said than done, try to just relax and look at the bigger picture – weeks, not days.

MILESTONES AFTER SEVEN MONTHS

After the seven-month mark, Ted was changing rapidly and it really felt like time was whizzing by. Weekdays were largely spent as they are now, juggling an extraordinary number of plates with Ted right at the top of the pile, but as a result weekends became sacred and the sole focus was spending it as a threesome.

Our first night away

While this is always our default setting these days, we did realise that catching up with friends had fallen completely by the wayside. They all understood, of course, but when an invite came to join a good group of friends that we hadn't seen in a very long while, we decided that we should bite the bullet, especially as it involved a night away in a posh hotel in Hampshire. Mum and Dad jumped at the chance to baby-sit overnight and so off we set, child-free for a whole 24 hours. It was our next milestone, **our first night away**.

We took our time getting ready while sipping an ice-cold G&T, already experiencing the complete antithesis of what we had gone through over the last seven months. It was heaven. In a new dress with make-up done, hair done and legs shaved, I walked hand in hand with Charlie towards the drinks reception. Charlie had made an effort too, and both of us looked more like our pre-baby selves than we had in a very long time. We chatted, we caught up with friends, we drank, we showed photos of Ted, we drank some more, we danced, we belly-laughed, we danced some more and even had an impromptu sing-song around a piano. It was brilliant fun, but at just gone 2am we were done. That was the sum of the equation of a rare night away, plus copious amounts of alcohol drunk quickly due to excitement at sudden freedom, which equalled two parents who are too drunk to have sex and need to lie down until the room stops spinning. Well done us. My new lingerie didn't even see the light of day as I fell asleep in my clothes, shoes and all.

Our first thought when we woke was Ted, and although Mum reassured us that he was absolutely fine, I had an overwhelming urge to hit the road. We couldn't even finish our breakfasts. I was fidgety and impatient. I needed to see my little boy, and I needed to see him *now*. Had you described this new version of myself to the woman I was 18 months ago, I would have laughed and made some quip about how 'we would definitely take advantage of Mum and Dad and have a huge lie-in and get back after the baby goes to bed on Sunday night', but that was the opposite of what I wanted to do. The weekend had definitely blown the cobwebs away, reconnecting with friends had been great and we've promised ourselves that we'll have another night away on our own soon, but in the meantime, it turns out that we're just as happy to stay at home.

'Smiles are a baby's secret weapon, they bring them out just as you are at breaking point. I think you have to make your own milestones, by that I mean don't focus on what other babies are doing at a particular time. Make note of the wonderful change happening to yours. It has been really reassuring to me to see how unique she is!' Liz

SITTING UP... AND CRAWLING

By seven months Teddy was sitting up on his own, which was a revelation! In the lead-up to this stage, he had become frustrated with being horizontal and putting him to lie on his back was like setting off a grenade. Sitting up unaided meant that I could put him down with his toys on the kitchen floor and he would happily play while I did some chores. Perfect. Suddenly, life seemed easier, but instead of just enjoying that phase Charlie and I were foolish and greedy and wanted more. We should have embraced this brief but wonderful spell when our baby could sit up and entertain himself but was stuck to the spot, meaning observing was easy. But foolishly we encouraged crawling. It was a rookie mistake.

It all started when Charlie received a video from one of the other dads in our NCT group. The video showed footage of their baby expertly speeding on all fours around their kitchen. Papa bear's competitive edge kicked in, and before he knew it Teddy was on his stomach with Charlie at eye level with him, trying to teach him how to crawl. That first video started a chain reaction, and over the coming weeks, more videos of different babies in the group hit our WhatsApp thread. Nobody would have dreamed of saying out loud that this was a competition, but it most definitely was. Every day we would set Ted on the floor and tempt him with his favourite things, the remote or a mobile phone. Nothing was working and even Jess, our nanny, was under strict instructions to coach him during the day. It all backfired when, one Thursday afternoon as I sat rehearsing for *The One Show*, Jess sent us a video. The subject was 'Look at him Go!' My heart sank, knowing what I was about to see. There he was, my baby, crawling for the first time without his parents there to see it and applaud him. I was grateful to Jess for capturing the moment – she was super excited too and wanted to share it with us – but it didn't make me feel any better. Charlie's response echoed how I felt. 'Wow, clever boy! Feel like we should have been there to see that. (Sad face).'

Short of being with your baby every single minute of every single day, there is no guarantee that you'll catch these milestones. There's no solution. Some you'll witness, and others you won't: it's just life.

Now that Ted is on the move, nothing is sacred. I used to be able to sit him in front of the cubicle while I had a shower and he would happily watch the water cascade down the glass, but one morning I opened my eyes post-shampooing and realised that he had disappeared. Soaking wet, I flew out of the cubicle, and still there was no sign. Our bathroom is small and options are limited, but finally I realised that he had opened the airing cupboard door and crawled inside, and what I found was a very sweet-looking exorcist, covered in gloopy green stuff having opened and emptied a spare bottle of shower gel all over himself.

'The milestone of my kids actually being able to read and write is pretty massive. It feels like a giant leap in terms of their brain and ability. My son is in reception now and it brings joy to me to see him writing his name and reading signs phonetically. They've gone from being a baby, toddler, to an actual reading, writing, member of society. Next stop...university!' Selfish Mother

We did as thorough a health-and-safety assessment as we could following this incident and have made the relevant adjustments, but Ted, like all babies, has an uncanny knack of finding the one plug socket or rogue hazard that went unnoticed. It suddenly feels that parenting, just as we thought it was getting easier, has gone up a gear.

'As a busy mummy to two beautiful boys (Bobby 3 and Ted 1) and an infant school teacher, sometimes it's hard. The single most useful piece of advice given to me by one of my super duper more experienced mum friends is this: EVERYTHING IS JUST A PHASE I cling onto this, whether it's a period of sleepless nights, difficult dinner times, wriggling out of car seats, toddler tantrums... or one of the other many types of monkey business...It won't last forever!' Sophie

I'm guessing that next on *our* agenda is teething, as Ted is nearly ten months. Either that or walking. When he's not crawling, all he wants to do is hold on to our hands as leverage and pull himself into a standing position. This new obsession is manageable during the day, and goes a long way to help banish any bingo wings, if I'm honest, but at 3 or 4am, when he's wide awake and wanting to practise standing and walking, it can feel hideously laborious. With teething on the horizon, though, I'm guessing this phase is the fairer of the two. We're braced and ready for it. I'll let you know how it goes.

HELP,
WE NEED
SOMEBODY...

And you will, I guarantee it. Having a baby is the biggest game changer there is and even in the early days, having somebody around, family members or friends to stick a load in the washing machine or make you a cup of tea, is paramount to your sanity!

Our polite British natures mean that we are often compelled to politely decline help, but believe me, that would be a monumental error once there's a baby in the picture. When your mother or mother-in-law offers to come and stay 'to help out with the little one' you agree enthusiastically, and find a way to never let them leave until it's time for your child to go to school. When friends pop over for a first glimpse of the baby and ask half-heartedly whether there's anything they can do to help, you say yes please and write them a long list.

The nature of the type of help you need will change over the course of the first few months, from practical help that family and friends can offer, to potentially professional help as you return to work and need someone to look after your child. Starting the process of looking for childcare that suits your child and your budget can be more daunting than the birth itself, and I hope that this chapter will go some of the way to enlightening you to what options are available, but first, let's celebrate the crème de la crème when it comes to unwavering support: the grandparents.

HELP FROM THE GRANDPARENTS

After Ted was born, my mum stayed with us for the best part of three weeks. Even as a 39-year-old woman, I struggle to imagine how I would have coped without her in those first few weeks, especially after Charlie had returned to work. In fact, I have never appreciated her more than I did then. She reassured me when I thought that I wasn't coping, she knew how to comfort my son when I was all out of ideas, she brought me porridge and tea every morning while I was breastfeeding, she quietly kept the washing ticking over and made sure the house was clean and tidy. She gave me time to recover from the birth and, above all, she gave me the confidence to become as good a mother to Ted as she had been, and continues to be, to my sister and me.

Those three weeks were without doubt the most precious of our entire relationship and I wept like a baby when the time finally came for her to go back to Dad in Carmarthenshire. Although she is too practical to dwell on it, I knew that saying goodbye that day pained her too.

Mum and Dad may live in West Wales, but they travel up and down the M4 so often that they could probably finance the toll bridge by themselves. They were very conscious of being equally as supportive of Charlie and me as they had been of my sister and her partner when they had their children. The big difference is that they live 40 minutes' drive from my sister, and nearly a four-hour drive from us, but Mum and Dad are tenacious, and over the last year, they have made the 250-mile journey seem insignificant, coming to visit on a fortnightly basis, and for that we couldn't be more grateful. The time, effort, love and support we receive from them in their role as grandparents is phenomenal and becoming a parent myself has taught me to love and respect them in a brand-new way.

While my parents are not exactly on our doorstep, Charlie's parents are even further away, 11,659 miles to be exact. They live on literally the other side of the earth in Auckland, New Zealand. Annabel, Charlie's mum, made the journey when Teddy was six weeks old and fell head over heels in love with her new grandson. It was an idyllic three weeks and for the best part she didn't let go of Ted, apart from when I needed to feed him, but the inevitable goodbye at Heathrow was one of the saddest afternoons I had experienced. It was always tough when they went back to NZ after a visit, but this time, Annabel wasn't just leaving her son, she was also leaving her grandson and my heart broke for the three of them.

How grandparents help

There are 14 million grandparents in the UK and two-thirds of them care for their grandchildren. Over the past two decades the number of children cared for by grandparents has risen from 33 per cent to 82 per cent. It's the obvious choice when it comes to childcare and, according to a study published in the

Guardian, children who are looked after by their grandparents showed more rapid language development and seemed generally more emotionally secure than their peers.

Here's the clincher though: grandparents are also saving working parents approximately £6.8 billion a year in childcare costs.

Yep, I'll give you a moment to digest that figure.

Money aside, it really does sadden us that Teddy won't experience having his grandparents on his doorstep, but we are typical of so many couples who moved to London or other big cities as single people, and ended up meeting someone, marrying and raising a family there.

As well as distance, there is also another significant reason as to why some late-bloomers are unable to ask their own parents to care for their children. Couples in their late thirties and forties sometimes find themselves having to juggle looking after young children with caring for elderly parents who are ailing. It's without doubt one of the more cruel side effects of late baby-making. On top of that, both parents are often working full- or part-time, and with childcare costs having risen by 50 per cent since 2010 how on earth are they meant to survive?

We may be living the demographic paradigm, but some would argue that with all these pressures on thirty- to forty-something parents, we may not be necessarily living the dream.

> 'As I'm the main earner we knew I had to go back to work at eight months. Due to finances I had to go back full time. My husband's job is also full time....with no family help this

was more than scary. Nursery full time was an option - and one I feel guilty about every day. Finding a nursery was hard - so many have very long waiting lists and it turns out I put Fran on the waiting list for her current nursery when I was six weeks pregnant. Juggling is hard - my work is intense and I'm studying as well. I'm always letting people down. I wouldn't change having my baby for the world - what I would change is flexible working and help for young families. There's an expectation that grandparents are around to help - with us that's not the case....so we have a huge nursery bill.' Rachael

THE COSTS OF CHILDCARE

Nobody said that having a child was cheap, but, with childcare costs spiralling out of control, short of selling a kidney, what are your options?

Many parents in England breathed a huge sigh of relief last year when the government announced that they would provide 30 hours of free childcare for children over three. (It seems a long way off for us now but it's good to know that it'll be waiting for us when the time comes.) However, what about families who don't live in England, my mates in Wales, for example, or families who have two children under the age of three who need full-time care? Lots of parents who are 35 and older end up with a small gap between the first and second child as they simply don't have the luxury, biologically, of extending the gap. It's more common than ever for a couple to have a child who, let's say, has just turned two and a six-month-old baby.

Well, the good news is that there is some help at hand.

The first of which is the government's tax-free childcare scheme.

- The state will contribute 20p for every 80p that parents spend on childcare, with a maximum of £2,000 a year per child.
- Parents who work more than 16 hours per week and earn over £100 per week are eligible, but earnings must be less than £100,000 annually.
- Parents apply by opening an account online that they pay into and which is then topped up by the government to cover the cost of a registered carer.
- This system will eventually replace the original childcare voucher system, but the good news is that you can still apply for childcare vouchers until April 2018.
- Under this scheme parents can claim up to £55 per week, tax-free, towards their childcare, and for basic taxpayers it adds up to about £1,000 per year.
- This can double if both parents sign up to the scheme.

So which is best for you? Well, generally, tax-free childcare makes more sense if you are a parent to two or more children as it offers savings per child, per year. Childcare vouchers are likely to be better if one parent doesn't work at all or if one parent earns over £100,000 per year.

Even with this help available, dual-career couples are enduring the biggest parenthood penalty in living memory as childcare costs in the UK are currently higher than anywhere else in the world, costing parents on average a third of their income.

Many couples, having done their sums, come to the conclusion that financially they're simply better off with one parent working while the other stays at home to care for the child. You could, however, consider shared parental leave. You see, an employed mother is entitled to 52 weeks of maternity leave and she can share 50 of these weeks with her partner. (The first two weeks are mandatory.) Parents will be paid by their respective employer when they receive shared parental leave pay, currently at £139.58 per week. Even the partner of a self-employed mother may be cligible in some cases. A great option for some dads who are ready for a career break and who want the opportunity to be a stay-at-home father.

Who stays and who goes back to work is a tough call to make, especially as child-raising in your late thirties and forties often coincides with the peak of your professional career. Dutch economist Lans Bovenberg has coined the phrase 'The Rush Hour of Life', which is pretty spot on to describe what most of us feel that we're experiencing.

'We started early in our mission to find the right nursery as I didn't want to be disappointed and go on a waiting list after finding the right one for us all. I arranged four or five visits and went off to have a look around. I narrowed it down to two and my mum came to view them too so I could get another opinion. My husband also viewed the final two nurseries. My mum always picks up on things I wouldn't think of asking (through being an experienced mum I guess!) and the questions she had really helped me. Like what happens in an emergency? What is the menu for food? How do you record the learning taking place? When is this recording of info completed? (some nurseries produce fab books and folders with photos etc). We settled on a nursery where a) we loved the baby room and staff b) it was in a super location and c) it was recommended to us by friends. And to be honest it just felt right. They made me feel at ease. Settling in sessions for both mummy

285

> and baby are really important. They helped a lot. William started at 11 months. He went for two days a week to start with then three days after about six months. I do know that we are really lucky with childcare in that I have Mondays off and my parents do one day.' Caroline

What options do you have?

So if the decision is that both parents will work, the next task is to decide which childcare option would work better for your family. Having been there recently, let me warn you that it's tricky terrain to navigate. First you really need to work out the basics:

- Do you need part-time or full-time care?
- How many hours a day will you need help?
- What's your budget?

Let me give you some idea of costs to start you off.

Nursery

A full-time nursery for a child under two, which means 50 hours a week, is approximately £222.36 per week, rising to £275.83 in London.

I went to see many nurseries for Teddy, and naturally some met his needs better than others. For example, many nurseries didn't particularly cater for babies under one, and while they had cots they didn't have a quiet room that was dedicated to babies, which in my opinion is of paramount importance so that infants get the rest they need.

The other problem for us was flexibility. We were looking for four half-days and while that was possible in most nurseries

I visited, they closed at 6.30pm, meaning that due to our work hours, Charlie and I would never get home in time to collect Teddy.

It's worth noting that these establishments have strict policies where time-keeping is concerned and implement heavy fines for lateness. The most severe I came across was £25 for every five minutes past closing time. So, you should be very sure that you can collect your child within their hours if you're thinking of signing up. I'd be bankrupt by week three!

Flexible working hours can go some way towards lightening this particular load. Any parent with a child under 17 who has been with the same company for six months can ask for compressed hours, flexi-time or a job-share option, which can work around childcare and specifically, nursery opening and closing times but, sadly, none are an employee's right. It's up to your boss, so you may want to float the idea before you disappear on maternity leave to make sure that they have sufficient time to get their head around it and be able to support you.

'Flexible working is not a revolution; it's simply about evolution in a digital realm that's willing and ready. Nearly nine million people in the UK say that they want to work flexibly, but don't have the option. This is despite the fact that since 2014, every employee who has been in their job for more than six months has the right to request flexible working. Flexible working doesn't mean slacking off or working less, it means finding hours that suit your life and how you best work. It also makes economic sense for companies – when parents drop out of work because their working hours are no longer tenable, the economy loses their knowledge and tax revenue. Flexible working is better for staff, and it's better for profits. When you're asking for flexible working be confident – remember, this is not you admitting that you can't cope, or that you no longer care about your job. Come with a plan ready, one that outlines exactly what you are asking for, and how flexible working will actually benefit your employer.' Anna Whitehouse, AKA Mother Pukka

Nanny

If a nursery isn't for you, you may consider a nanny. It's a more flexible option as your child will be cared for at home, and it could be more suitable for very young babies. Also, hours can be arranged at your discretion.

However, this one-on-one service inevitably comes with a bigger price tag. Depending on experience, a part-time nanny could set you back between £237.50–£375 per week, and a full-time nanny £512 per week plus tax and national insurance. It's also worth remembering that you will need to pay holiday and sick days. Outside London, the cost would typically be around £1,600 per family per month for a full-time nanny, working ten hours a day, five days a week, including tax and national insurance. It's worth considering if you have more than one child as a nanny charges per hour and not per child.

There's no denying that having a nanny is an expensive business, but about a third of the cost could be saved if you considered a nanny-share with a friend or local family.

If you can swallow the eye-watering cost, the next step is to find the right nanny for you. This is no easy feat, and some friends have admitted that finding the right husband was easier!

My tip would be to avoid using an agency. Although they will ensure that all the relevant checks are done and will do most of the leg work for you, you will end up paying a commission that's upwards of £1,000. Yep, it's a lucrative deal for the agencies and a bitter pill to swallow for you.

We decided to swerve an agency, but bear in mind that it can be a daunting process, especially as you have no prior experience and don't really know what questions to ask or even what qualifications you're looking for. It's a bit of a stab in the dark, to be honest. Typically, we left it to the very last minute. I started interviewing just a fortnight before I was due back at work, which could have been way too late had we not been as lucky as we were to find our nanny Jess as soon as we did.

To avoid unnecessary panic, start sooner, even before the baby is born, to avoid stress and to allow you the freedom to enjoy your maternity leave without having the worry of finding childcare.

Our first port of call was to make enquiries among friends who already used a nanny. Sure enough, some of their nannies had friends who were between families and so I arranged to meet them over a coffee.

The hardest thing was knowing what questions to ask as I had never employed a nanny before. I interview for a living and still some meetings were a bit awkward, like a date when you don't have very much in common, and I would find myself oversharing. I knew from these awkward meetings that these candidates weren't right. Just remember that they will be at your house a lot and ultimately will become pretty much a member of the family so you need someone you can at least chat with.

Alarm bells would sound if the candidate didn't seem interested in finding out about Teddy. Some wouldn't even ask his age or what sort of baby he was, nothing. They were automatically struck off the list.

Bear in mind that any number of nannies can have the right qualifications and tick all the boxes on paper, but you will know when you've found 'the one'. It's hard to describe, but it will be a feeling deep in your gut, so try not to settle on anyone until you experience that feeling or you'll find yourself back at the drawing board quicker than you can say 'Mary Poppins'.

I met six nannies in total and two really stood out. One of the girls needed a live-in position as she couldn't afford to rent in the area, and although we toyed with the idea, ultimately we decided that we wanted our privacy in the evening. Truthfully, I would find it stressful having to constantly be polite and not being able to have a full-on argument in case a third party was privy to it. Also, we didn't want to have to give up our only guest room permanently as our parents need the bedroom when they visit. Live-in nannies can work well for families who have plenty of space and it can be a cheaper option as you're providing board and lodgings as part of the deal.

We are delighted with our Jess, who's originally from New Zealand but is travelling in the UK. She's hard-working, flexible, mature, punctual, forward-thinking... the list goes on, but, more importantly, she adores Teddy, as he does her, and even though it still kills me to walk out of the door in the morning, I'm comforted by the fact that Teddy is happy and I know he'll be well cared for. On top of caring for Ted, Jess is also kind enough to help us out with light household chores, some of which we negotiated at the time of employing her – it's important to be very clear about what you expect and to note that in a contract.

'I was lucky that my employers agreed my application to reduce from 5 days a week to 3 days. I was even luckier that both sets of grandparents agreed to help out with childcare so we only needed to find 1 day a week of paid childcare. It was important for me that my daughter went to someone who would give her the attention and love that I did, and that she felt safe and secure. I decided to pick a childminder as I felt like the close relationship was more important. She was fab and my daughter settled in straight away. However the biggest drawback of using a childminder over a nursery is if the childminder is ill or on holiday you have to find cover, or take a day off work. I did find it difficult having to take time off work for childcare issues, I always felt guilty and I guess a bit frustrated, but we made it work between us all. Working full or part time and juggling childcare can be very stressful. I feel like I had it easy in a way because my husband worked from home so he was able to do all the drop offs and collections and I just had to sort myself out most days! I couldn't imagine working full time and having to sort all of that out on top.' Jenny

Au pair

If the cost of a nanny is out of your budget and you have a spare room, you could consider a more affordable au pair. You will need to provide free food and lodging, plus a minimum of £75 per week in pocket money, and in return you can expect 25 hours a week of care plus two evenings of baby-sitting. While an au pair may have some childcare experience and qualifications, they are not a nanny and have usually come to the UK to learn a new language and to experience a foreign culture.

How to find a nanny or an au pair?

Although you can certainly ask around friends for nanny or au pair recommendations, like we did, another good place to start your search for whatever help you require is websites like **nannyjob.co.uk** or **childcare.co.uk** where you can specify what position you're offering, punch in your postcode and find suitable candidates. Each candidate's qualifications and experience will be included on their profile. These sites are great places if you're looking for nannies, childminders, baby-sitters, au pairs or indeed maternity nurses, if you decide that you need some help during those never-ending nights in the first few weeks. These sites also include suggestions of the type of questions you should ask when interviewing your prospective carer, making the process a lot more manageable.

Making decisions about going back to work and finding the right nursery or person to care for your brand-new baby is probably one of the toughest and most important tasks you will face in the early years. Without peace of mind that your baby is safe and well cared for, you will not be able to concentrate at work and so the whole thing is futile. Being as happy as you can be with the care that you have in place is paramount. Yes it's expensive, but spending money on quality childcare should be a priority above everything else, and ultimately it will make the tough decision of returning to work more palatable. Get stuck in, and start your search as early as possible; it'll make things so much easier in the long term. A good support network of people you can trust implicitly will help everything else fall into place. Good luck!

JUST THE ONE?

> 'I was 42; we knew that if we wanted a second, it would have to be sooner rather than later. I've felt a lot more relaxed this time, and if the breastfeeding doesn't work, I'm not going to push myself. I think because I was older I put so much pressure on myself to get it right. Its tough though – we had our first through IVF at 41, now I'm 42 and due with the second, again through IVF. Back-to-back IVF was never the plan, but since when does life ever really go to plan?' Clarissa

We're nearly at the end of the book now, but having discussed the highs and lows of being a first-time parent, there is still one piece of uncharted territory. You know what's coming.

Just four hours after Teddy's birth we were already fantasising about a little brother or sister for him. The oxytocin was flowing, we were high on life, obsessed and awestruck by this little being who had just come into our world and relishing our new roles as parents. At that moment, we would have naively, yet happily, had another straight away. However, five days into our new life, constant worrying, never sleeping and painful breastfeeding meant that the afterglow faded somewhat. We were back on a more realistic keel. This is a common trait in new parents; blinded by love and flooded with hormones, we momentarily crave more children than we can probably cope with. It's this love and optimism that essentially gets us through the first few days of adjusting to our new chaotic and all-consuming lives with our babies.

Contrary to what some believe, there is no hard evidence to support the notion that the longing for a child, be it your first or your fourth, is biological and not just psychological. This may go some way to explaining why some men and women never feel the urge to have a child, and good on them; they're free to continue to enjoy life-long lie-ins, impromptu nights out, fast sports cars, immaculate houses filled with white soft furnishings... the list goes on.

The rest of us know that we would rather live in houses filled with colourful plastic toys, drive unstylish people carriers, survive on little to no sleep, have to plan a night out with military precision – and all because we desperately want to be part of a nuclear family and, in many cases, want to replicate the same set-up we grew up with.

As we know, this urge doesn't disappear just because we can't find the right partner at the right time, but if you've wanted three children all your life, meeting someone to play the parent game with at 35 makes this tricky.

On the flipside, some of us will know older parents who got overexcited during a rare night away from the children, got on the wine and came home with more than they bargained for. Obviously, not all unplanned pregnancies happen like this, but it's happened exactly this way for three couples I know. The new addition is always loved and cherished, but the initial news can cause extreme shock and a lot of soul-searching as parents worry about the financial impact of a latecomer, how he or she will affect the dynamic of the family and whether, as parents in their late thirties or forties, there is enough energy left to care for another newborn and go through that beautiful yet brutal period all over again.

So, say that you've had your first child in your mid-thirties or early forties and you want another baby, how soon should you consider trying again?

- Should you rush into it because, after all, time is ticking and no one is getting any younger?
- Or should you wait, because your body has already been through the mill and perhaps needs more time to recover than if you were in your twenties?
- Or should you cut your losses, be grateful for what you have and stick with one?

At three months after Teddy's birth, I had already started an internal dialogue with myself about when would be a good time to start thinking about having another one. I didn't share it with Charlie at that point, worried that it was a bit premature and that the sleep regression we were experiencing with Teddy at the time wouldn't be a great marketing ploy for another.

However, it was Charlie who brought it up first. We were discussing flying to New Zealand for Christmas when he simply asked, 'Can you fly before the three-month mark if you're pregnant?'

I nearly spat out my tea, but instead, gathered myself and tried to sound casual. 'Yep, I think so,' a revealing smile playing at the corners of my mouth.

He started laughing. 'See, I knew you were thinking about it.'

Busted. There was no use denying it. I tried to press him on his thoughts but, non-committally, he just said that he didn't think we should leave it too long. That was enough for me.

CONTRACEPTION? OR NOT?

At your six-week check, your GP will ask what method of birth control you want to use going forward. Like most new mothers, I looked at my doctor blankly. 'Contraception?' I repeated, as if it was a term I'd never heard of. I don't know about you, but sex was not on the agenda that soon after stitches. They were contraception enough in themselves, and considering whether I wanted to go back on the Pill was the last thing on my mind.

After discussing my worries about going back on the combined pill given my age and the fact that we would ideally like more children, the GP prescribed the mini-pill, assured me that it would have no long-term effect on my fertility and that I could just stop taking it the minute I wanted to get pregnant. I collected the prescription from the pharmacy on the way back to the car and instantly stuffed them in a drawer in my bedside table and forgot about them.

'I put so much pressure on myself to continue to exclusively breast feed when my little boy wasn't putting on enough weight, which I regret now. I turned to combination feeding and it was a revelation to be able to let other people feed him and give me a break and to see my hungry boy satisfied! I later found out that while I was still breastfeeding I had fallen pregnant again. A devastating shock. Before I'd had a proper period, before I'd returned to work and before any of us were ready. We were in deep turmoil over whether to keep the baby and what the right thing was to do for our evolving family. I am now four weeks away from giving birth again, 13 months after my first baby and about to embark on the journey of #wingingit with two under two. Wish me luck! (I will totally bottle feed sooner this time round when I feel the time is right rather than put pressure on myself).' Felicity

SEX AFTER BABY

Slowly, but surely, old wounds healed and it was time to get back in the saddle, if you know what I mean. Let's be frank and honest here. Having sex for the first time after giving birth, especially naturally, is daunting. You will imagine all sorts of grotesque scenarios, and worry about it all feeling a bit different in a 'loose' sort of way. My advice? Just do it. Get it done and move on. It's actually fine, pleasant even. Yes, your boobs are a bit different, squidgier, and there's a bit more wobble on both sides (new dads have no time to go to the gym either and often display a little post-pregnancy pouch) so just lie back, because you'll have no energy to do anything else, and try to enjoy yourself. It was a relief to get the first one in the bag, to know that the important bits felt the same and that we could be 'us' again and not just a mother and a father. We were back in the game. Admittedly, the 'game' is played less often these days as opportunity is at a premium, but you will find unexpected gaps in the schedule and you can always play the game very, very quickly.

GETTING BACK TO THE SECOND BABY QUESTION...

With sex back on the table, well, not literally, we're not that adventurous these days, I thought about those mini-pills nestled in my drawer. Should I take them for a few months, just to give us breathing space? But at 39, why would I risk delaying things by taking a contraceptive? It was a conundrum. You see, despite the GP's reassurance, I was still sceptical about taking any sort of pill. Every pill works by producing a hormone that thickens the mucus, making it difficult for sperm to get through the cervix. With the mini-pill, the effect only lasts for 24 hours and that's why you have to be so careful about taking it at the same time every day, whereas the combined pills are much more user friendly but more potent hormone-wise.

Luckily, I got pregnant very quickly the first time after coming off the combined pill, but I really wasn't sure whether I wanted to risk interrupting my body's natural rhythm this time around. What if my periods didn't return to normal for 12 or even 18 months, which is common in some women? There were so many considerations. First and foremost was the fact that although we had had no problem conceiving Teddy, there was no guarantee that our second go would be plain sailing. The flipside of that was if we did fall pregnant easily, would my body be able to cope, and would it carry a second child as safely a second time around so soon after delivering Ted?

The official advice is to wait at least 18 months before getting pregnant the second time around, whatever your age. Research suggests that beginning a pregnancy within six months of a live birth is associated with an increased risk of premature birth, placental abruption, low birth weight and congenital disorders. It also showed that having a second baby less than two years after the first can increase the risk of autism in second-born children, with the risk being higher for children born within a year of each other.

Also, common sense tells us that a woman is depleted of stores after delivery, even more so if she breastfed, and so the official view that women should be back to normal six weeks after birth is unrealistic. A famous study by Dr Julie Wray of Salford University back in 2012 concluded that women needed a year to recover both physically and emotionally from childbirth.

How soon is too soon?

So what to do? I didn't have an answer and so I went with my gut feeling and left the mini-pill in the drawer, and our fate in the lap of the gods. I mean I was still breastfeeding first thing in the morning and last thing at night, so that was a natural contraceptive anyway, right?

Not necessarily!

I had stopped breastfeeding exclusively when Teddy was three months, at the end of April, and then I stopped completely at four months. One morning, mid-July, I realised that I still hadn't had a period. Back to Google: 'How long should you wait for a period after breastfeeding?' The answer was six to eight weeks after breastfeeding although it can take months before your period is regular. Right. I slowly processed the information. Shit. I ran to find our calendar and started counting weeks. Eleven weeks since I breastfed exclusively! Shit! You can guess what the next calculation would be... how many weeks pregnant would I be if I was? I was sweating now. Ten weeks pregnant! More googling of 'early pregnancy signs', which is anything and everything if you want it to be, and then the ultimate calculation: how much gap would there be between Teddy and the new one? Oh my God. Thirteen months! Thirteen months! I spent the next week fluctuating between a daydream where Ted and his little brother or sister would be so close in age they would be the best of friends and spend every waking hour playing together, and a nightmare where I imagined Charlie and me like headless chickens changing two sets of nappies, having two cots, having to fill a small lorry every time we went to visit my parents in Wales because of all the baby paraphernalia. I felt sad that Ted would only have us to himself for not much over a year. I worried that I would be off again on maternity leave when I'd only just got my feet back under the table – and how would the news of another baby so soon be met by my bosses? There was one other big question, and one that I'm sure most new parents who are blindsided by love for their firstborn ask themselves: could we love another as much?

My concerns were completely futile as my period eventually decided to turn up the day we went on holiday. Of course it did. I started taking the mini-pill haphazardly with a plan to stop in October, meaning that even if we fell pregnant immediately, there would be 18 months between Teddy and the next tiny Thomson. We're thinking positive and while it may be a small gap, and not what we might have chosen had we done all this a decade ago, the bottom line is that we don't have the luxury of time and having a family is our number one goal. Everything else can be sorted.

What if it doesn't happen?

But what if it doesn't happen? And, let's face it, it might not. I will never forget the poignancy of what Anne Robinson, of all people, once told me in her uncomplicated way: 'Do it right the first time, you may not get a second chance.'

I know that I've been luckier than most in life. I have a supportive and loving family and husband, a job I absolutely love, a comfortable home and, most importantly, a healthy and happy little boy who is the apple of my eye. So are we happy with our lot? My head says yes, absolutely. I can't believe that Teddy is ours and we are beyond grateful that we have him. He has added joy in quantities that we didn't know possible and if this is it, then so be it. Charlie and I had a frank discussion about it as I wrote this chapter and he was fervently sure that while a second child would be amazing, we are already complete as a family of three.

After a lot of soul-searching, I'm unable to be as pragmatic as him, unfortunately. While my head is all too aware of how lucky we have already been, my heart secretly still longs for a little brother or sister for Teddy and I'd be disappointed to say the least if we weren't blessed with a second child. What can I say? I feel horrible admitting that I would be sad when plenty of close friends haven't even fulfilled their dream of having one child, but I always imagined having at least two.

'We conceived with IVF, and I have to admit I have worried that trying for a second would somehow be taking someone else's chance – like we've had our luck once, shouldn't that be enough?' Sarah

There is no denying how strong and all-consuming that desire for a first child can be, yet until you have experienced caring for your own child and formed that unique bond, you don't have the full picture. In a sense, you don't really know what you're missing until you've been there. The fertility battleground is brutal whatever your situation, but what's certain is that couples who are experiencing difficulties conceiving for the second time tend to be reticent about sharing their anguish, silenced by society's attitude that 'one is better than none', especially if you're past 35. I imagine that it's a very lonely place for couples who are quietly suffering miscarriage after miscarriage, too embarrassed to share that they're upset because although they have a healthy child they want another and the fact that it is not happening is breaking their hearts.

My close friend fell victim to this and when I asked her why she hadn't confided in us sooner, she simply looked at me and said, 'Well, I'm 41. I shouldn't be sad that it's not working when I've already got Annie.' My opinion, for what it's worth, is just even though we are starting later, we still have a right to dream.

'We'll see you next year,' was the last thing the midwife said to us, with a knowing smile, as we left the maternity unit at the Queen Charlotte hospital with Teddy. I looked at her in disbelief – it really was a bit soon to be thinking about doing it all over again – but who knows, she might have been right. I really hope so.

The start of the best adventure of our lives.

EPILOGUE

'It really does feel like the best job in the world.' Vikki

In the midst of all the chaos and confusion of being a new parent it can be hard to remember to laugh, which is often the one thing that will save you. With that in mind, I would like to share one final anecdote.

It was the May bank holiday, and Charlie and I decided that it was time for Teddy's first visit to the zoo, despite the fact that he'd just turned 17 weeks. I know, we were a bit keen, but we'd romanticised about days out like this since the very early stages of my pregnancy, and with no other plans, we decided to play grown-ups and do our first day trip. We managed to get ready in record time for us, and having packed 70 per cent of the house into the boot of the car, we set off at 1.04pm. We still needed to work on our timings.

The day lived up to the fantasy in every single way. The cloudless sky was a zingy cobalt blue and it was the hottest day of the year so far. We happily ambled through the gates, carefree and optimistic, with a whole precious afternoon of togetherness stretching out in front of us.

As we navigated our way around the various enclosures, we watched, smitten, as little Ted gurgled happily, absorbing all the new sights and sounds of the zoo. With the sun smiling on us, we posed for a thousand selfies (I never thought I'd be one of those parents, but hey, here we are) in front of the gorillas, the giraffes and the penguins before lazing on the shaded grass for a picnic while Ted devoured his milk. We were living the family-day-out dream – that was, until we arrived at the rainforest enclosure.

Bearing in mind that it was around 27 degrees, I strongly suggested that we swerve the hot and humid greenhouse, concerned that it would be too uncomfortable for Teddy. The promise of sloths was too tempting for Charlie, who is a frustrated zookeeper, and, in a blink of an eye, the pram had disappeared through the heavy plastic entrance curtains and into the Amazon, leaving me to follow in his wake.

No sooner had I made it through the moist, sticky curtains, than I saw a tiny tamarin monkey leap from his perch and make a beeline for the pram, jumping onto the base, his scrawny yellow tail curling around the wheel. With my heart in my mouth, and everything in slow motion, *Matrix*-style I jumped towards the pram to save Teddy, shouting 'CHAAAAAAAAARRRRLIEEEEEE' as I went. He was way too engrossed in the sloths to notice or hear me. With Teddy safely in my arms, I watched in horror as the furry creature noticed that the zip of the changing bag was open and chanced the one arm he had (he was called Bandit) and jumped right in. He delved deeper and deeper, rubbing his monkey body all over the contents of the bag, the cool bag containing Teddy's milk, all the nappies and every piece of spare clothing that we'd brought with us.

The irony is that my pre-parent self would have found this whole episode very amusing. I would have been made up that this monkey had chosen us and I would have considered closing the zip on the bag before anybody noticed and taking the little fella home. However, times had drastically changed. All I could think about was germs! I imagined the bacteria spreading all over our belongings, the monkey contaminating everything in his path.

'Come on little rascal, out of there please,' I tried to coax him in my most monkey-friendly voice but nothing was working. All I could see was his bottom and long tail poking out of the bag, his top half ensconced in the contents. Charlie was at my side now, unhelpfully videoing the whole episode.

Bandit in our bag!

With Teddy getting heavy and my patience wearing thin, I took action.

'Excuse me,' I said to a bloke in a London Zoo-branded polo shirt. 'Can you please get your monkey out of my bag?'

Fruit and various sticks were fetched but Bandit remained steadfast in the bag. I was full on sweating now, the humidity suffocating and all 16 pounds of Ted sticking to me. A crowd gathered to watch, and it was only a matter of time before we heard. 'Hey, you're off *The One Show*... this would make a bloody hilarious piece.' A titter erupted but people were still unsure of whether the person in front of them was in fact the girl off the telly, so frizzy was my hair.

I needed to get myself and Ted out, but Bandit wasn't playing ball; he just sat, unmoving, laughing at us.

It took all the persuasion of the actual zookeeper to finally get our tamarin friend out of the bag and back into the tree. We fled for the exit, cooking in our own skins and gasping for air.

We planned to wash EVERYTHING the minute we got home, but with bank holiday traffic doing its thing, what should have been a relatively short journey turned into *Ben-Hur*. Roads were closed, people were angry and the sat nav was losing its shit. An hour in, and Ted's wailing became deafening – it was well past his feeding time. We turned down a side street near Paddington, new-parent angst dictating our irrational decision. As soon as the engine was switched off, I turned around to reach the changing bag that was in the foot well behind the driver's seat, but froze in my tracks as I realised that the whole thing was covered in monkey DNA and the only hand sanitiser that we had was inside the bag.

Ted was hysterical and desperate times call for desperate measures. Using our fingertips only (because obviously that makes all the difference), we managed to get the milk and a clean bottle out of the cool bag that had been sealed inside the bigger bag and fed Ted. We expected the cries to ease away, but after a few snotty gulps, he started up again. I picked him up to comfort him and felt a familiar warm, wet stain across his back. I turned him over, knowing what I'd see and, sure enough, the pungent yellow excrement was trickling down his chubby legs. He needed a change, and fast.

As all parents will know, this is a tricky manoeuvre in the car, especially now that the changing mat that was in the changing bag, had traces of Bandit all over it. Placing his grey hoodie on his lap and Ted on the hoodie, Charlie gingerly set about the task, pulling wipes from the pack, trying not to touch the pack at the same time and using the nappies that were in the zippered section, thus free from contamination, while not letting them touch anything else in the bag. The lesson we learnt the hard way was to always carry extra supplies in the car, separate to the bag, just in case. Our glove box is now always fully stocked! Ted survived the ordeal and fared better than the hoodie, which now also desperately needed a hot wash.

After much cursing at the monkey, we finally got home and pandemonium ensued as operation clean-up began. We first bathed Ted and put him down, then it was anti-bac spray on the pram in large quantities, and finally, the flinging of everything and anything that may have touched said pram into a 90-degree hot wash, including the changing bag and all its contents. Throwing in a tablet, I walked away victorious.

We sat in the kitchen with our Friday night supper of pizza and wine reminiscing about the day, already seeing the funny side of the monkey episode. We were off to Norfolk to stay with some friends the following morning, so I emptied the washing machine before we went to bed, hoping that Ted's essentials would dry in time.

As I went to open the door of the machine, I realised very quickly that something was wrong. It was like looking at a snow globe. I opened the door and out spilled chunks of what looked like tissue that was heavily coating every item that had been in the drum. At first I assumed that I'd left some tissue or maybe some cotton wool in one of the pockets of the changing bag, but on closer inspection, it was more pulpy and there was loads of it.

One item at a time, I emptied the machine until I discovered something red and plasticky stuck to the back of the drum. My heart stopped. It couldn't be, could it? A feeling of impending doom washed over me as I realised exactly what had caused the mess in the machine.

In my panic to eradicate any trace of monkey, I had forgotten to check every compartment in the changing bag and had shoved it in complete with Ted's RED BOOK. All the precious health records that had been taken since his birth had been obliterated, boil-washed into oblivion, with the remnants mostly stuck to Charlie's grey hoodie. It was a colossal fail.

'What the hell is going on here?' A quarter of an hour later, Charlie came to check on me, wondering what was taking so long. He found me sat on the floor in front of the machine, surrounded by what looked like fake snow.

His first response was: 'Oh no, what's happened to my hoodie?' Typical. Then he came closer and spotted the melted red bit of plastic in my hand. We just looked at each other. I couldn't find the words to explain that his son had no medical records left, so I waited as the penny dropped. Eventually and incredibly, 'You haven't, have you?'

Guilty silence followed by lots and lots of tears and snot. I was gutted. It was sad that all the recorded weights from his birth through to the first three months were gone. It's a pretty archaic system so there was no electronic backup – this was it. I felt like a lousy mother.

The phone call to the health visitor was interesting. They never answer the phone so I left a message. 'Hello, this is the mother of Edward Thomson, I'm afraid that a monkey got into our changing bag and to cut a long story short, I've boil-washed the red book and there's nothing left. Could you please call me back to arrange a new one? Thanks.'

We did get a new one eventually, handed to me by the health visitor in a waterproof folder. Most of the information could be recovered, like which immunisations he'd had, but lots of notes that were made at his time of birth were missing. I did my best to remember what I could, filled it in and grudgingly moved on, ready for the next disaster.

At least it makes for a good story.

Being a parent is a relentless marathon that we are all lucky to be running. You'll feel stressed, overwhelmed, frustrated, elated and everything in between, but so long as your child is safe and well, everything else is just detail. Try as much as you can to have a laugh; it makes things so much easier.

And remember to smile. It'll make you look less tired and it's your baby's number one favourite thing.

Oh, and one last thing: never agree to write a book in your first year of parenthood.

EPIC FAILS!

Elliot

'Neither of us wanted to give our son Max a dummy. We'd both thought it wasn't a good look, possibly unhygienic and linked to all kinds of dental and speech problems. So we resisted until he was six months old. After many nights comforting him (because of a milk issue he was having, causing him stomach-ache) we relented and discovered that a dummy kept him calm, quiet and helped him get to sleep. In other words - we gave in. But he kept losing it in his cot in the middle of the night and waking up screaming. So we came to a solution. We figured if we put TWO dummies in his cot then that would double his chance of finding at least one of them in the night. Simple maths... Our son is now three years old. Every night since we made that stupid decision he has gone to bed with two dummies, one in his mouth and one in his hand – and he is incredibly emotionally attached to BOTH of them. If he loses either one of them in the night he wakes up and cries. We simply doubled our chances of a sleepless night. Just call us the dummy dummies....'

Rob

'I should first say I'm a retired police officer; cops are lucky because we retire comparatively early so, at 51, my wife and I had a baby daughter. Maddison was born in the month of my retirement from 30 years as a detective. The pregnancy and birth was uneventful and 18 months later we decided to bestow on baby Maddison the gift of a little brother or sister, but one has to be careful what one wishes for. Two years almost to the day later, my wife gave birth to triplets! Maddison is now almost seven and the triplets almost five, and me? I'm now nearer 60 than 50 but in my head, I'm 22! When the triplets were babes, Maddison was just under two. My wife works evenings and one particular evening lives fresh in my memory. Around 6ish I was alone, as usual, with all four; triplet Ben had his usual sludgy mess of wet, fresh poo and I was busy changing him on the waist-high changing table. As you probably know, babies have a way of moving their arms and legs at critical times in such a way as to touch, throw, splash or otherwise facilitate human poo to go where you don't want human poo to go and Ben was no exception. I began trying to hold his perpetual motion leg while completing the nappy change with my free hand. At this most critical time I heard banging coming from the lounge, I looked up and could see triplet Lucy hitting the television screen with a toy wooden block. Sadly my cries of "stop it Lucy" were met with a vacant look as she continued her quest to bust the TV. Simultaneously Maddison shouted from the downstairs loo, "Daddy I've had a poo." She had made it to the toilet and was now demanding my attention. At that very moment there was a clatter and a metallic crashing noise coming from the kitchen. Triplet Francesca was up to no good. So, what is a dad to do? Thirty years' police training kicked in, decisions had to be made and risks needed assessing. Quickly I removed Ben's offending nappy and gently placed him on the floor. On doing so I ran into the lounge to save the TV from Lucy's destructive intentions. Finally Maddison, and bum-wiping duties. Now, I've discovered that little girls' knickers, when they're around the ankles or lower leg, can have a trampoline-like quality. As I attended my eldest little cherub I could see the fabric of her knickers was taut and resting upon it was yet another lump of, yes you've guessed it... poo! The challenge now was to carefully manoeuvre the knickers to enable her to release one leg at a time, while ensuring the poo did not spring from the knickers and catapult towards me. I did it! Third issue solved and all was well – however there was still a disturbing noise to investigate, coming from the kitchen. I found Francesca sat on the floor among an assortment of saucepans and other utensils with a cheeky mischievous smile. Phew! Nothing too serious and within minutes peace and harmony once again returned to the Jones household with Dad cuddles all round. Feeling quite pleased with myself, an hour or so later, I allowed myself the luxury of a cup of comforting tea. Reaching for the kettle I thought, "What's that smell?" The answer summed up my life with four children under two at that time; next to the kettle and alongside a piece of cake was a pair of girls' knickers and a rather unpleasant piece of human waste! I had completely forgotten to dispose of the offending poo and worse, had left it where I had put it. Parenthood has a way of normalising human behaviours those without children can scarcely understand or believe!'

Karen

'Epic parenting fail.... When my baby boy was a week old I thought his fingernails were looking a bit long. I took the freshly bought special baby scissors and promptly cut the very top of his finger off. Five seconds later I'm dangling a screaming baby over the kitchen sink trying to get his finger under running water. He's 13 now with five perfect fingers. At that moment though I never thought I'd get him past the first month! Parenting is the hardest and the best thing ever!'

RESOURCES

GENERAL
BabyCentre www.babycentre.co.uk
NCT www.nct.org.uk
NHS www.nhs.uk
Mumsnet www.mumsnet.com

FERTILITY AND CONCEPTION

Fertility
British Fertility Society
  britishfertilitysociety.org.uk
NHS www.nhs.uk/Livewell/Fertility/
  Pages/Fertilityhome.aspx
IVF www.nhs.uk/conditions/ivf/
  getting-started
It's definitely worth looking up your local
  IVF support group too.
Information for LGBT+ couples
www.nhs.uk/Livewell/LGBhealth/Pages/
  Havingchildren.aspx

Ovulation and pregnancy apps
BabyCentre www.babycentre.co.uk/
  mobile-apps
Clue www.helloclue.com
Glow glowing.com
Ovia www.ovuline.com

PREGNANCY
Antenatal appointments www.nhs.uk/
  Conditions/pregnancy-and-baby/Pages/
  antenatal-appointment-schedule.aspx
Alcohol www.nhs.uk/conditions/
  pregnancy-and-baby/pages/alcohol-
  medicines-drugs-pregnant.aspx
Food www.nhs.uk/conditions/pregnancy-
  and-baby/pages/foods-to-avoid-pregnant.
  aspx

LABOUR
Hypnobirthing hypnobirthing.co.uk/
  what-is-hypnobirthing
Water birth www.nct.org.uk/birth/
  use-water-birth-pools-labour

BABY
Baby blues www.nct.org.uk/parenting/
  baby-blues
Post-natal depression www.nhs.uk/
  conditions/post-natal-depression

Breastfeeding
Breastfeeding Network www.
  breastfeedingnetwork.org.uk
Helpline: 0300 100 0212
Kelly Mom kellymom.com
La Leche League www.laleche.org.uk

Bottlefeeding
www.babycentre.co.uk/a752/
  bottle-feeding-basics

BABY-LED WEANING
www.babycentre.co.uk/a1007100/
  baby-led-weaning
Gill Rapley, *Baby-Led Weaning*, Vermilion,
  2008
Food for toddlers/baby Nikki Duffy, *River
  Cottage Baby and Toddler Cookbook*,
  Bloomsbury, 2011

WORK
Maternity pay and leave www.gov.uk/
  maternity-pay-leave
Paternity pay and leave www.gov.uk/
  paternity-pay-leave

CHILDMINDERS, NANNIES AND AU PAIRS
Find a registered childminder
www.gov.uk/find-registered-childminder
www.care.com
www.childcare.co.uk

INDEX

First and foremost I would like to thank every single one of you that took the time to share your honest and eye opening accounts of parenthood. Your stories floored me and have helped start conversations about really important stuff that nobody had really spoken about before. I'm sorry we couldn't use every one, but I hope you know that each story helped shape this book in some way. I hope you enjoy the end result.

Thanks to Paul, Laura and especially my editor and fellow mum, Natalie. And many thanks to Lorna, Roman, Eva, Maddie, Alex, Carl, Chris, Amanda, Jack and Talah, who came down for the shoot, as well as all our expert contributors to the book.

To my friends, especially Lou and Marge, you have listened to endless hours of chat about this book. Always with enthusiasm and ideas. I know it must feel like you've lost a friend this year, but we'll always have Palma. Caru chi!

Thanks to the NCT mums. You have been a lifeline over the last year.... and now I can get stuck in with play dates again.

The hugest thanks is for you, Mam and Dad. I can't thank you enough for teaching me what parenting is really about. I have been so lucky to watch true masters at work over the years, and although I'm still learning, I'm learning from the best. If I can give Ted even half of what you've given Jen and I, he'll be winning.

Jen, thanks for the endless tips. You are my inspiration and are a mother like no other. I hope to be like you when I grow up although you're my little sister. You're the best!

To Charlie, without you, this book would definitely not have happened, both literally and practically . Thanks for your support and enthusiasm and for going along with my brain wave of doing this in our first year of parenting. I know it was tough at times. You are the best teammate I could have hoped for and the Tedster and I love you very much.

Teddy (my muse) the happiness you have brought me in this first year has been indescribable. You are loved more than you'll ever know and I sincerely hope that this book will be a source of great entertainment to you when you're old enough to read it.

Here's to the rest of our lives xxx